Successful Copywriting In A Week

Robert Ashton

The Teach Yourself series has been trusted around the world for over 60 years. This series of 'In A Week' business books is designed to help people at all levels and around the world to further their careers. Learn in a week, what the experts learn in a lifetime.

Robert Ashton is a social entrepreneur and established business author. His books have been translated into 18 languages and sell in almost 100 countries around the world. He attributes his success in business and in print to his ability to translate complexity into clear, compelling copy. In this book Robert shares the secrets of effective, persuasive writing.

Teach® Yourself

Successful Copywriting

Robert Ashton

www.inaweek.co.uk

Hodder Education

338 Euston Road, London NW1 3BH.

Hodder Education is an Hachette UK company

First published in UK 2003 by Hodder Education

First published in US 2012 by The McGraw-Hill Companies, Inc.

This edition published 2012.

Copyright © 2003, 2012 Robert Ashton

The moral rights of the author have been asserted

British Library Cataloguing in Publication Data: a catalogue record for this title is available from the British Library.

Library of Congress Catalog Card Number: on file.

The publisher has used its best endeavours to ensure that any website addresses referred to in this book are correct and active at the time of going to press. However, the publisher and the author have no responsibility for the websites and can make no guarantee that a site will remain live or that the content will remain relevant, decent or appropriate.

The publisher has made every effort to mark as such all words which it believes to be trademarks. The publisher should also like to make it clear that the presence of a word in the book, whether marked or unmarked, in no way affects its legal status as a trademark.

Every reasonable effort has been made by the publisher to trace the copyright holders of material in this book. Any errors or omissions should be notified in writing to the publisher, who will endeavour to rectify the situation for any reprints and future editions.

Hachette UK's policy is to use papers that are natural, renewable and recyclable products and made from wood grown in sustainable forests. The logging and manufacturing processes are expected to conform to the environmental regulations of the country of origin.

www.hoddereducation.co.uk

Typeset by Cenveo Publisher Services.

Printed in Great Britain by CPI Group (UK) Ltd, Croydon, CR0 4YY

Contents

Introduction   2

Sunday   4
Focusing your message

Monday   20
Using layout, pictures and colour to make words
memorable

Tuesday   36
Writing effective letters

Wednesday   52
Making advertising work for you

Thursday   70
Communicating clearly with the media

Friday   88
Preparing promotional print

Saturday   106
Composing proposals and presentation visuals

Surviving in tough times   117
Answers   121

Introduction

It's strange to think that there was a time when only the privileged few could read or write. The rest of us relied on the spoken word. Storytelling was used to pass knowledge on from one generation to the next.

Now, most of us are literate and use the written word to gather information and inform decision making. Unlike speech, writing communicates your message to people you cannot see and may never meet. It means you can influence more widely; it also means you must take care not to make assumptions about your reader.

Successful copywriting is constructed from carefully selected words, each with a clear purpose. It is written to prompt feelings, thoughts or actions. It is clear, concise and at times comforting. It is also comprehensible, even to those not yet confident users of your language.

Reading this book, and following the techniques it introduces, will make you a more effective writer. Expertise in grammar is not needed as all the necessary jargon is simply defined and, anyway, some forms of business writing deliberately ignore rules. This book is for people who want to write for results. Successful business writing makes you:

Better understood

More influential

Easier to understand

Able to lead others

More likely to achieve your goals

SUNDAY

Focusing your message

Today we will explore some of the basics. We will build our understanding of what will make your writing more appealing and effective. Remember that although few read business copy for pleasure, it should be a pleasure to read.

Effective business writing captures attention, arouses interest and prompts action.

By the end of today, you will understand:

Why you must have a clear goal

How to structure any piece of writing

Some relevant jargon and what it means

Words guaranteed to 'hook' your reader

SUNDAY

MONDAY

TUESDAY

WEDNESDAY

THURSDAY

FRIDAY

SATURDAY

Focus on the result

Before starting to write your copy, jot down what you want to happen as a result of your words being read. Try to prioritize them as follows.

As a result of reading my copy my audience will:

- **Know** – what I have set out to tell them
- **Think** – that what I am describing is relevant to them
- **Do** – something as a result of having read my words'

For example, in a memo that asks people to attend a meeting, you want them to:

Know – when and where the meeting is, how long it will take and what will be covered

Think – about what they can contribute to the discussion, and also think that there will be a clear benefit to be gained for them if they attend

Do – let you know if they can attend or, if they cannot, who perhaps can come in their place.

If there are eight teams in your company and you need six people to turn up, representing at least five of the teams, to drive through the decisions your meeting makes, you can measure the success of your copy by how many teams are represented.

Now think about some pressing goals that you need to achieve through others. Try to list the objectives in terms of what you want people to **know**, **think** and **do**. It should make focusing a lot easier. When you start writing, it will also make it a lot easier for your reader to work out what you want him or her to **know**, **think** and **do**. The clearer your message, the easier it will be understood.

Structure to succeed

Even if your job means you never meet a customer, it could be argued that your business copy needs to sell. This is because business writing has to be persuasive and, as we all know, sales copy can be the most persuasive of all. In our example above, in which we seek to arrange a meeting, we have to persuade people to attend. They will no doubt have other things they could do instead. Remember, too, that in writing your words are substituting for your voice. If you are writing sales copy, your words are making a 'sales presentation' and need to follow the structure of a sales interview. Let's take a look at the stages of the sales process, as this provides a useful structure for almost any business writing situation. It can work well, even if all you are selling is the need to stand away from the edge of a cliff.

1 Getting attention

Before your advertisement, poster, website, report or proposal gets read, it has to attract the eye of your target reader. It has to compete with interesting editorial, proposals written by your rivals and a whole lot else. Later, we will cover techniques that can help you do this, but for now, focus on the need to make your introduction punchy, relevant, exciting and able to communicate the nub of your message in a split second.

2 Make it personal

You will be familiar with those cheesy mailshots that mention your name, your address and something about you on every other line. These letters are written by experts. They know that using your name and referring to things you can readily relate to will make the letter personal to you. In a face-to-face meeting, most of those reassuring 'it's for me' messages are transmitted non-verbally, through body language. But you will not be standing in front of your reader, so your words have to do this for you.

3 Reasons to stay reading

Most people have a short attention span and are easily distracted. Your writing has to hold their interest. This is best achieved using 'benefits'. For example, we want you to keep reading this book because then you will become a better writer and will gain a healthy return on your investment. This is achieved by hinting at what is to follow in later chapters. This should help keep your interest and build your expectation. The back cover outlines what's inside and now that you are inside, you are being drip fed with hints that expand on those promised benefits. If you think back to the 'know, think, do' sequence, you can perhaps begin to see how you can introduce 'build up' to your writing, maintaining interest and keeping your reader with you.

4 Overcoming likely objections

You've grabbed attention, made it personal and now you've added some relevant benefits. Your reader will now be looking for the catch; that's human nature. What you have to do is pre-empt any objections by providing the answer before the doubt pops into their head. Project proposals are a good example of where this is really important. A section that breaks down the budget and resource implications and spells out the return is a great way to allay fears. You have to put yourself in the shoes of your reader, anticipate their questions and provide ready-made answers. This is why FAQ sections can be so useful.

5 Being believable

Business writing is a creative medium and you can say almost anything if you have the skill and technique to make your argument look credible. Your reader may realize this, so your text has to be underpinned with fact, or at least testimonial. To avoid litigation, particularly with advertising and promotional copy, you have to be careful to make only honest claims that can be supported. Remember, too, that operating manuals, personnel documents and even warning signs can, if they are misleading, land you in trouble. Consider the following statement.

SUNDAY
MONDAY
TUESDAY
WEDNESDAY
THURSDAY
FRIDAY
SATURDAY

> In independent tasting trials most people preferred cola brand X. We think your customers will prefer it too.

A good enough reason perhaps to stock brand X in your shop. Read it again. The independent trials were probably conducted in the street by a research company and there are methods you can use to influence tasting trials (for example, the first product tasted is often preferred to the second). Secondly, the writer only 'thinks' your customers will prefer brand X. If your customers prove to hate the stuff, you cannot sue the writer. Clearly the writer cannot say which your customers will prefer. The customers themselves need to make that particular decision.

6 Call to action

This is the most important part of your business writing for it delivers the result. You have to remember only to seek a realistic result and not ask too much of your reader. It is also important to encourage a response you can measure. For example, if your letter invites the reader to visit a business website, you have no way of relating the resulting 'hits' to the letter. Better to offer some incentive, or even set up a separate 'front page' for the promotion, so that you can track success.

Example

Now it's time for you to write something that illustrates this sequence. Imagine that you are selling coach holidays and are writing a letter to encourage your prospective customers to book early (to enable you to confirm your hotel bookings and boost your cash flow with their deposits). You've already sent out your new brochure and many of your regulars have booked. You feel that a well-written letter will encourage 100 more people who travelled with you last year to book again this year. You have a list, so each letter is mail-merged to make it personal. It might read something like this. The different stages 1 to 6 show you how the letter develops.

Dear Mrs Smith

(1) Don't miss your chance to enjoy another holiday with us next summer.

(2) I know that you really enjoyed your holiday with us last year, but am a little surprised that your booking was not among the many we have already received for next year. Some of our more popular destinations are already booking fast.

(3) As a regular customer, we would also like to reward your loyalty with a free welcome pack of speciality teas and biscuits (worth £10), which will be waiting in your hotel room if you book your holiday before the end of February.

(4) May I also remind you that we never discount our holidays at the last minute so there is no benefit in delaying your booking. This is because our holidays are carefully priced to be competitive with rival operators and also because we are usually able to book our hotels ahead of our competitors. We enjoy healthy discounts that enable us to offer you excellent value for money.

(5) I have enclosed a copy of an article in the Anytown Journal that compares our holidays with the major national coach tour companies. If you read it, you will see why we were so delighted when it was published; it's very flattering.

(6) Remember too that all you need to pay now is your £50 deposit to secure a place on the holiday of your choice. A booking form, reply paid envelope and list of holidays is enclosed. Please telephone me if you have any questions, otherwise I look forward to hearing from you soon.

Yours sincerely

Fred Greengrass

Tour Manager

Now you've seen an example, think of a situation where you need to write a business letter to a customer and see if you can follow the 1-to-6 format. Of course you will not necessarily have one sentence for each section as in this example; in fact you may be able to include more than one stage in a single sentence. What's important is that all six are adequately covered.

SUNDAY

MONDAY

TUESDAY

WEDNESDAY

THURSDAY

FRIDAY

SATURDAY

Some useful jargon

Many of the copywriting books you pick up are packed with jargon. This can make you feel unprepared and ignorant of the finer points of English grammar, rather than encourage you to experiment. I want you to focus on getting your message across, rather than trying to teach you English grammar!

That said, there are a few useful writing techniques I'd like to tell you about. I think you'll agree they can add flavour and impact to your writing. Business text can be dry as dust, packed with information and leave you no time to breathe, let alone savour the concepts the writer is trying to communicate. Truly effective writing paints pictures in the reader's mind, is rich, varied and leaves just enough to the imagination to make you think you drew the right conclusion all on your own. Here are some favourites to get you started. You might also want to hunt for others using reference books or the internet.

Metaphors – A metaphor is a figure of speech in which a word or phrase that usually describes one thing is used to describe something quite different. For example, 'All the world's a stage', which clearly it is not, but Shakespeare made his point that we are all performers in the play of life. Using metaphors enables you to inject subtle humour and, more importantly, to provide opportunity for your readers' imagination to 'kick in'. In a business context, describing an office as a 'hive of activity' is a metaphor. It implies, but of course does not say, that everyone is as busy as bees.

Similes – These can be really effective. It's where two essentially unlike things are deliciously compared to each other. This provides more opportunities for humour and fires the reader's imagination. For example, 'His desk was as cluttered as a shoplifter's pocket' or 'They sold like hot cakes'.

Alliteration – Commonly used in advertising headlines or in titles of proposals or reports, alliteration is where a sequence of words all start with the same letter or sound. Because of the way our minds work, alliterated lines catch the eye and are easily remembered. This technique can be used for the tackiest (Buy bumper basement bargains) to the most subtle of applications (Does dental decay daunt dentists?)

Enjambment – This is a term used by poets to describe the way the word at the end of a line leaves you hanging, eager to discover what is revealed by the line below. Very useful when working with designers and you need to determine where to put line breaks in a piece of text. For example:

> 'We know you will be delighted by how our range of lipsticks will enliven your smile.'

Oxymorons – Oxymorons are combinations of words that on their own contradict, but together say something rather special. They are often best used to emphasize key benefits, those points you want your reader to know, think or do.

> With our database you can organize chaos!

Homophones –These are also used to emphasize your key points. Homophones are words that sound the same but are spelled differently. For example, son and sun. 'You know our sauce comes from a reputable source.' These make the reader stop and think.

Practice

It is not necessary to remember all of these terms; it is enough to practise them and adopt those that suit your personal style and the type of business you are in. An estate agent will use different words in different ways to a travel agent. Before you move on, though, spend a little time trying out the following exercise. It will encourage you to experiment and push out the boundaries of your writing. You will soon see which techniques you enjoy using and which irritate you. Why not try them all, then focus on those you are most comfortable with? You can always add others later.

Imagine that you are managing a leisure centre. You have to write copy that will influence the general public, but you also have to motivate your team and encourage them to follow good practice. Write some simple statements that might help explain this, using:

- Metaphor – for a poster that sells swimming lessons
- Simile – for a memo encouraging gym staff to keep the equipment clean
- Alliteration – for the day's specials on the cafeteria blackboard
- Enjambment – on promotional T-shirts for a community 'fun run'
- Oxymoron – to describe the 'employee of the month'
- Homophone – for a 'keep fit' slogan

Don't worry if you find this quite challenging; it will get easier with practice. Remember, too, that this is all about making your business writing more effective, so ask others to review your words and give you honest feedback.

Hooking your reader

As already stated, the best way to win the favour of your reader is to flatter them. This clearly is easier if you have more information, for example in a single letter or document intended for a small audience. Here you can use the reader's name, or at least their organization's name, and make the message personal.

With direct mail to some extent, and certainly with advertising, you will know little about your reader unless they decide to respond to your message and identify themselves. In this situation, it is good to remember some basic social rules.

For example, we all like to be acknowledged and the most powerful word you can use is 'you'. Use phrases such as 'we know that you will enjoy our barbecue sauce', which sounds much more appealing than 'our barbecue sauce is enjoyed by millions'. The reader is not really interested in the majority view; they only want to feel that it will taste nice to them.

Summary

Today you have started your journey from literate individual to competent copywriter. You will have recognized the importance of clarity and focus in your writing. You have also practised planning exactly what you want your reader to **know**, **think** and **do** as a result of reading your words.

Then, you looked at the sequence in which information should be given. Your reader needs encouragement to start reading, to stay with you and then, ideally, to actually give you some measurable feedback.

Next, you were introduced to some perhaps initially complex terms that describe interesting ways in which you can arrange words to boost their effect. That was the only jargon you will encounter in this book. You will find with practice that you will naturally adopt some of the techniques and forget what all of them are called. That's fine and really not a problem.

Lastly, you were reminded of the importance of making the message personal to your audience. You can best do this by using people's names and, wherever possible, words like *you* and *yours*. You will have a chance to cover some of these points again as you now move on to look in more detail at some different situations where your growing skill as a business copywriter will help you to achieve more in your job.

SUNDAY

MONDAY

TUESDAY

WEDNESDAY

THURSDAY

FRIDAY

SATURDAY

Fact-check (answers at the back)

SUNDAY

MONDAY

TUESDAY

WEDNESDAY

THURSDAY

FRIDAY

SATURDAY

1. When people read your copy you want them to:
   a) Ask others to explain it to them ❏
   b) Understand exactly what you mean ❏
   c) Use a dictionary to check out the big words you use ❏
   d) Be impressed by your grasp of English grammar ❏

2. Good business writing is best done when you are:
   a) Tired ❏
   b) Angry ❏
   c) Calm and focused ❏
   d) Late ❏

3. When writing business copy you should focus most on:
   a) The words ❏
   b) Your audience ❏
   c) Your objective ❏
   d) Yourself ❏

4. As a result of reading your words, you want people to:
   a) Know, Think and then Do ❏
   b) Show it to a colleague ❏
   c) Remember for future reference ❏
   d) Get annoyed and ring you to complain ❏

5. You need to pitch your business writing to be:
   a) Understood only by your target audience ❏
   b) Filled with jargon to demonstrate your specialist knowledge ❏
   c) So simple even a 5-year-old would get the message ❏
   d) Open, accessible and relevant to everyone who might read it ❏

6. Structure and flow are vital because:
   a) It makes it easier for you to write that way ❏
   b) It makes it easier for people to read ❏
   c) You need to take your reader on a logical journey ❏
   d) The author of this book has said so ❏

7. You want people to keep reading to the end because:
   a) It's interesting and relevant and they want to see what you're suggesting ❏
   b) Every paragraph makes them laugh out loud ❏
   c) They can't believe your cheek and audacity ❏
   d) It's a good way to pass time ❏

8. Metaphor adds colour to your writing. Which of these is a metaphor?
   a) A school of dolphins ❏
   b) A street of houses ❏
   c) Three wise men ❏
   d) A hive of activity ❏

9. Alliteration helps people remember headlines because:
   a) All the words start with a different letter ❏
   b) All the words start with sequential letters, e.g. D, E, F, G ❏
   c) All the words start with the same letter ❏
   d) All the words are from different languages ❏

10. Your business writing should be
seen by the reader as:

a) For them   ❏

b) About them   ❏

c) About you   ❏

d) For the good of the
    organization   ❏

SUNDAY

MONDAY

TUESDAY

WEDNESDAY

THURSDAY

FRIDAY

SATURDAY

MONDAY

Using layout, pictures and colour to make words memorable

Before you start writing, it is worthwhile spending some time considering how people read. You need to recognize the significance of shape, layout, illustrations and even the texture of your document. Your reader will be unwittingly influenced by the way in which you present your writing, as well as by the words that you use.

Today, you will:

Discover how the eye scans a page and what this means

Understand the value of pictures and know where to find them

Consider some typographical techniques that help words stick

Learn what makes words memorable, especially product names

Appreciate why you should always tell it like it is

How people read

You could be forgiven for assuming that our eyes start scanning the page from the top left-hand corner. Indeed, as you reflect on your eyes' journey to this point on the page, you may not realize that before starting to read the words, your eye will have quickly scanned the whole page before choosing where to begin. The cartoon, for example, will almost certainly have, quite literally, 'caught your eye' and been viewed before you read a single word.

A lot of research has been carried out into the way that information transfers from the page to the reader's brain. In fact, in the advertising industry it is a science. You do not need to study too much of the theory, however. Your goal is simply to become a more effective copywriter, so here are the basics.

Imagine that your document, advertisement or even business card is divided into four equal quarters or quadrants. X marks the spot your eye will automatically go to first on the page. Experts call this the 'primary optical area'. The eye will then travel up towards the top left-hand corner, perhaps to establish where the page ends, then follow the Z shape as depicted below.

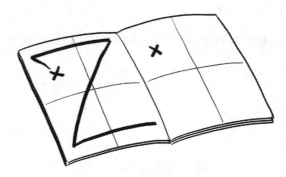

This visual flow, or eye-path, tells you where you have to position the most important, arresting, attention-grabbing thing you have. That way, the reader's interest is aroused and, without even realizing it, they will slow down and look more closely at what you have prepared for them.

Now take a look at some advertisements because this is where the phenomenon is most commonly seen. Take a ruler and pencil and draw that Z shape over the top of the ad. Can you see how, often, the message builds as you follow the line of the Z? A picture usually covers at least the primary optical area and often more of the page. You are then led to the headline, which often starts with a distinctive letter, symbol or even starburst to mark the corner of the Z. The headline then feeds you the key benefit. The long diagonal takes you through the picture again and the detailed text, called 'body copy' in the trade. The Z ends with what is termed the 'call to action'. A telephone number, coupon or shop address. It will be particularly useful to remember this on Wednesday when advertising copywriting is covered in some detail. Today however, we're focusing on shapes and colours, not words.

Using pictures

There is an old Chinese proverb that says that one picture can save 1,000 words and this is largely true. If you have studied neuro-linguistic programming (NLP) you will be familiar with the concept that some people are more receptive to pictures than others. Though the simple fact is that everyone will look at the picture first, then read the words. It makes sense therefore to use pictures, diagrams and graphs whenever you can to get your point across. They always improve understanding and speed comprehension. There can be very few occasions when an illustration of some kind cannot add impact, weight and sense to your writing.

Another useful nugget from the world of advertising is that we like to see pictures of people. This is not surprising when you think that the first object we learn to recognize as a baby is usually our mother's face. Conversely, adults are most affected by child-like images. This is why cartoon characters often have large heads in relation to their bodies. It both makes the whole body seem baby-like, vulnerable and appealing, and also places more emphasis on the facial expression.

Here are some useful points to consider when selecting pictures to illustrate your work.

WHAT	WHY
One or many	One large picture has more impact than several smaller ones
Colour or black and white	Colour is not a panacea. Contrast and content are more important
People	Faces get noticed. Men look at men, women at women
	Use different people to illustrate the range of your audience
Backgrounds	The best pictures are close-ups with no background
Oddities	A small oddity can catch attention. For example, adding an eye-patch to a beautiful girl
Endorsement	Your branded van in front of Buckingham Palace will imply more than the same van photographed in a multi-storey car park

Finding good pictures

Inevitably, you will always want pictures that you cannot easily find. It is worth spending a moment thinking about where you can source good pictures to illustrate your writing.

Here are a few tips on finding good pictures:

- Ask your customers and suppliers, where appropriate, to provide photographs
- Always carry a camera at work to capture those spontaneous opportunities
- There are many online photo-libraries from which you can download images
- Graphic designers have an eye for good pictures and can also draw for you
- You can buy royalty-free DVDs packed with all kinds of pictures

And now a few things to avoid:

- Do not use clip art unless you really have to. It's naff and suggests you've not really tried very hard. Be different
- Do not infringe anyone's copyright and 'steal' images. Ask first
- Wherever possible, get permission to publish someone's photo in advertisements
- Remember that some people are easily offended so avoid controversial images

Graphs

Too often you will see figures presented in columns and tables, with accompanying text that interprets and comments on the main trends or statistics. A graph can show the key trends and issues in an instant. It all depends on the level of detail you need to get across. Fortunately, most spreadsheet packages can produce graphs for you at the touch of a button. If figures form a major part of your business communication, consider developing your spreadsheet skills so that you are comfortable using the graphics as well as the formulae. It will enable your reader to grasp the key trends in a flash. Remember too that graphs need to be positioned on the page where they will be seen first, to prepare the reader for the detailed figures which follow.

Colour

When you are producing printed documents, colour inevitably adds to the cost. With text, however, more colour does not necessarily mean more impact. In fact if your work appears too kaleidoscopic, people will avoid, rather than read it. Although most offices now have colour copiers and colour printers, you do not have to use all of the features available to you. Colour is best used to:

● highlight key points, perhaps coloured text for a key passage in a lengthy tract
● prioritize or show relative risk. You can use 'traffic light' colours to indicate preference, risk or even relative cost
● illustrate detail, perhaps in technical or scientific drawings and documents

Experts have estimated that advertising responses can be up to 50 per cent higher when colour is used rather than black and white. But equally, sometimes a message needs the starkness and simplicity of black and white to grab attention.

Practice

You are now halfway through Monday's chapter and before leaving pictures and shape to move on to words, their shape, form and arrangement, you may find it helpful to do an exercise that will reinforce the points covered so far. Take a pile of magazines, newspapers and journals that are relevant to your work or perhaps a favourite hobby. Now take an A4 piece of paper, some scissors and glue, and create a montage using just pictures to convey a positive message about your chosen subject. Remember to use the 'Z' to position your pictures in a logical sequence and to use people as well as objects. A good tip is to use faces to show feelings and objects to inform, so you might have a smiling face and a fast car, or a sad face and a crashed car. When you have finished, show the picture to someone you trust and see if they get the message.

Presenting words

Now that you have a better understanding of how important images are, it is time to get back to words. In fact, words and sentences are also viewed as images. When most of us read, we do not study each letter and form the word in our mind. Instead we scan the line and use the shape of the whole word to identify it and translate it into an image or a perception in our mind. The art of arranging or formatting text is called typography and, as with pictures, most of the research into this subject relates to advertising. Since it could be argued that all business copywriting is advertising – for it seeks to 'sell' a concept, idea or product – it is appropriate to consider how good typography can give your writing a winning edge.

Fonts

With everything we create on our computer, or have produced by a designer or printer, we have a choice of typeface, or font. Some are old, trusted and venerated, others new, contemporary and stylish. Many organizations have an 'in-house font' in which all corporate communication must be produced. This then becomes part of the organization's brand, and manuals are produced that define how every document, printed leaflet and advertisement should look. Banks and insurance companies are typical in this respect.

For you personally, it is often a question of personal taste and preference. Fonts fall into two main styles. 'Serif' fonts are where the letters have little tails or hooks on. These serve to bounce your eye from letter to letter, word to word. It is said that serif text is easier to read than plainer 'sans serif' (without serif) text. Take a look at your computer. The chances are that you can choose a font such as Arial, which is sans serif, or Times New Roman, which is a serif font. Try composing some text in a number of different fonts and see which you find easier to read.

Typographic tips

There are several easy-to-remember tips that can aid the legibility of the text that you create. Remember that your reader is not necessarily going to be someone you know. They may be older, younger, possibly speak English as a second language, or have poor eyesight. The more you can do to help them, the more likely they are to read what you have written for them. Here are five of the most popular typographical tips.

- Starting a block of text with a drop capital increases readership. That is where the first letter is much larger than all the rest
- Keep sentences short, with no more than 16 words
- In letters and proposals, use 11- or 12-point type and 1.5 line spacing
- Use bold and italics to highlight key points. Colour can also be used
- Widows are single words that have spilled over onto the next line. They make text blocks less block-like and daunting and help the reader (Designers, however, do not like widows and try to remove them!)

Choosing words

We have looked at how the words should be arranged so it is time now to choose the words you are going to use. You may have studied English at university or be an avid crossword fan. If you are, you will have a wide and varied vocabulary. What is more important, however, is the vocabulary range of your reader. If your writing is too simple, it can seem patronizing; too complex and it will appear arrogant and aloof. You have to strike a happy balance between the two extremes and use words that your reader will understand. It's what I've tried to do with this book.

Of equal importance is not to repeat the same word many times. This makes your writing boring to read and does little for your credibility. Buy yourself a good thesaurus and use it regularly to find commonly used alternatives for the words that keep cropping up. You can also buy and download computer thesaurus packages. These enable you to highlight a word, explore alternatives and replace with the one you prefer. These are not expensive and have a far wider vocabulary that most word-processing software. Less relevant, but fun all the same, are the websites that send you a new word every day (for example www.dictionary.com). Subscribing to these can broaden your general vocabulary, as well as brightening your day.

Making new words

In a marketing environment, the creation of new words to name products and services is an industry in itself. As marketers know, giving something new a name helps to define it and to bring the benefits into clearer focus. Some of the most memorable brand names, for example Oxo, Aviva, Axa and Elle, are what is termed palindromes. That means they can be read the same way backwards as well as forwards.

As an exercise, why not try to think of some new names for products or services that your organization produces. Remember that old products can be cheaply refreshed with revised names, new packaging and very few new features.

Tell it like it really is

Rather like the policeman who knocks on the door to give you bad news, the more you beat around the bush, the more frustrated and anxious your reader will become. It is always better to be explicit and say exactly what you mean. You can then expand on the point in the following sentence. This is infinitely better than working up to the punchline. Here are a couple of examples:

> Our detergent works best at lower temperatures, saving you up to 20% of your fuel bill. This is because the product is packed with modified enzymes that are able to digest stains at a lower temperature.

> Kennel-X in your dog's bowl will make his tail wag faster. The specially formulated crunchy nuggets are both tasty and keep teeth and gums healthy. A healthy dog is a happy dog.

Note that in both examples, the key benefit message is contained in the first, short sentence. The words that follow expand on the message and justify the claim.

Practice

It is now time for you to write some text. Find those cut-out pictures you used earlier to make the montages and now write some copy about the message within your montage. Make the first sentence explicit and then support it with two more that emphasize and illustrate the benefits you are seeking to convey. Remember, too, from Sunday the importance of using the word 'you' to make the message personal to the reader. Next, put your words on screen and experiment with different fonts. Can you see how to bring it all together?

Summary

You have now explored the visual aspects of creative writing. You should have a much better grasp of how people read and have practised ways in which you can make it easier for people to get your message. In all Western cultures, where we read from left to right, the 'Z' pattern outlines the route our eyes follow when we look at a page. Pictures can say so much more than words, but do need supporting words to explain exactly what it is the picture is saying. In fact it has been proved that captions under pictures are a good way of reinforcing advertising messages. Spend some time looking at how others have presented their writing and reflect on the key points from today. The rest of this book focuses on composition and writing techniques used in specific situations so it is important that you are comfortable before reading on.

SUNDAY

MONDAY

TUESDAY

WEDNESDAY

THURSDAY

FRIDAY

SATURDAY

Fact-check (answers at the back)

1. Layout and presentation are:
a) Immaterial – it's the words that count ❑
b) Vital if the reader is to complete the page ❑
c) Useful, but only if you can afford to hire a designer ❑
d) Complicated, so let's not go there ❑

2. Readers always look first at the:
a) Top right ❑
b) Top left ❑
c) Bottom left ❑
d) Bottom right ❑

3. Pictures and illustrations make your writing:
a) Easier to read and understand ❑
b) No different, but they're nice to have ❑
c) Confusing – this is business writing, right? ❑
d) Overly complicated ❑

4. Pictures are best used:
a) On their own; the reader will get what you mean ❑
b) With a caption to make the relevance obvious ❑
c) Sparingly because they take up valuable space ❑
d) Like a cartoon strip, with hardly any words at all ❑

5. In general, people prefer to see pictures of:
a) Products ❑
b) Places ❑
c) People ❑
d) Food ❑

6. If you do a lot of business writing, it's always useful to carry a:
a) Notebook and pen ❑
b) Camera ❑
c) Pocket recorder ❑
d) Chocolate bar, as writing can be hard work ❑

7. Graphs help people interpret complex figures. Graphs should appear:
a) Before the figures to set the scene ❑
b) Instead of the figures because detail's rarely important ❑
c) After the figures, in case people are still confused ❑
d) In the text with the figures in an appendix at the back of the document ❑

8. The best font to use for business writing is one that is:
a) Big and bold and maybe all in capitals ❑
b) The funniest one I could find in the system ❑
c) Clear and easy to read, ideally with serifs ❑
d) The default for my computer when it came out of the box ❑

9. When constructing each sentence:
a) Use lots of commas to break up the flow ❑
b) It's the content, not the length that matters ❑
c) Try not to exceed 16 words ❑
d) Be as short as possible ❑

10. When writing you should:

a) Say it like it is and be explicit and clear ☐

b) Build up the message and let your reader guess what you mean ☐

c) Play word games to lead your reader along ☐

d) Soften the message so as not to cause offence ☐

SUNDAY

MONDAY

TUESDAY

WEDNESDAY

THURSDAY

FRIDAY

SATURDAY

TUESDAY

Writing effective letters

We all write letters and perhaps more frequently, emails. In general, both follow the same protocols and rules, although emails are, by their very nature, faster and less formal.

As you work through this chapter, you can assume that everything you read applies equally to email as to the written letter. Where there are differences, I will point them out to you.

Today, you will:

Look at why you might write a business letter or email

See how writing can build business relationships

Consider how to balance formality with familiarity

Practise writing some letters for your business

Understand how email is both different from and the same as the written letter!

Email or letter – making the right choice

It's tempting to disregard the printed letter as slow and out of date. But think for a moment: how would you feel if you were invited to meet the Queen by email? Invitations to Buckingham Palace are always sent on a gilt-edged card, with the recipient's name hand written. These invitations are treasured and often remain on display long after the event. Sometimes, you want your business communication to have the same impact. Here are some ideas to get you thinking:

Letters are good for	Emails are good for
Making it clearly personal	Keeping in touch with people you know
Enclosing samples or literature	Directing people towards a webpage
Delivering praise or compliments	Sending information very quickly
Confirming an agreement because you can both sign and keep a copy	Enabling the recipient to share with others easily

A letter or email, unlike an advertisement, newsletter or brochure, is a personal communication between two individuals. Of course, in practice you may well send the same message to a number of different people.

Avoiding spam

We all hate unsolicited email, yet often we will send an email out of the blue. For your email to be seen as something other than spam, it must be clear to the reader immediately that this email is:

- addressed personally to just one person
- relevant to their situation
- credible

Why people will read what you write

Drayton Bird, one of the UK's most respected direct marketers, talks about the 'three graces' of direct marketing. These define well the advantages that writing a good letter can bring.

- **Personal** – You are isolating someone as an individual and demonstrating your knowledge of what makes them or their situation unique.
- **Proof** – You are showing that you want to build a continuing relationship with someone, respond to their feedback and meet their needs.
- **Profit** – You are giving them good reason to read and perhaps respond. By seeking their feedback you are engaging them in a two-way relationship. You are trying to help them as well as yourself.

The more succinctly your writing can deliver these 'three graces', the more successful your writing will be. It really is that simple!

Reasons for writing

Before exploring the different elements of a letter or email, pause a moment and make a list of the reasons you might have for writing to people. Think beyond the obvious and consider some you might not have thought of before.

Here's an example to get you started. Imagine that you run a restaurant in a small town. You want to get more people to visit your restaurant and, more importantly, to return time and time again. Here are some reasons you might choose to write a personal letter to your customers and prospects.

- To tell them about a special offer that will encourage them to come with friends
- To invite them to special themed events, e.g. wine tasting, Christmas, Mother's Day
- To let them know about new services, e.g. children's parties in the afternoon
- Because their birthday or another significant anniversary is approaching and you have a record of the date
- To contact people able to bring business to you, e.g. undertakers arranging a wake

The letter itself

Yesterday you considered some of the aspects of typography, such as the choice of font. You will also probably have a printed letterhead that provides your contact details and outlines what it is you or your organization does (and your emails will have this as a 'signature'). Today, we look at the content of the letter. Each presents an opportunity.

	Letter	Email
To	Get the name and address right. Avoid adding honours and qualifications unless you know the person expects it	Here it's obvious, but try to avoid the temptation of pasting lots of addresses in the 'To' box
Date	It is always important to date your letter. This avoids confusion	Remember that your email will arrive with the date and time you sent it. Even if it's at 1a.m.!
Salutation	Politicians always handwrite the 'Dear Mr Smith' salutation. It's quaint, but might suit your style. Choose either 'Dear Mr Smith' or 'Dear John', depending on the level of formality you feel is appropriate	Avoid using the word 'Dear'. It looks odd in emails. Instead, simply state their name, or even 'Hi John'. Remember that by its nature, email is less formal

	Letter	Email
Content	Get your points across in as few words as possible. Remember the 'three graces'	The same applies, but you can add hyperlinks to webpages to save words
Appearance	Use a clear font and make it as big as you feel comfortable with	Remember that many people view emails in 'plain text' so fancy formatting may get lost. Keep it simple
Sign off	'Yours sincerely' is always the best bet	'Regards' is the most common email sign off, but don't be inhibited if another word (e.g. 'Cheers') suits your style and business sector
Your name	Always type your name in full, i.e. Bill Jones, rather than W Jones. This makes it easier for the recipient to address you personally when they reply. If you have an unusual first name, it might be good to add a Mr, Ms, Mrs, Miss prefix to avoid embarrassment	Make sure your email signature is appropriate and take the time to edit for a specific email if not
PS	Can be irritating, but a good place to add a personal message to a mail-merged letter	A great opportunity to add a personal message to show this is not spam. (PS: I loved your last book launch, please count me in for the next one)

Never ever

Avoid at all costs those meaningless corporate phrases that too often creep into business writing. Perhaps the worst and most common is: 'Assuring you of our best intention at all times'. Please, please use more imagination.

Now to write a letter

Imagine that you are running a motor dealership and want to keep in touch with your customers. Think first about why writing regular letters might be profitable for you. Make a list. Here are a few to get you started:

Reason	Benefit
To check that customers are happy with their new cars	Pre-empts complaints Collects testimonials for your advertising **Demonstrates** that you **care**
To tell them how regular servicing reduces running costs	Promotes your servicing workshop **Shows** you can save them **money**
To invite them to a new model launch	Gets them into your showroom/ new car Maintains personal contact **You** show them new things **first**
To congratulate their car on its imminent third birthday	Reminds them that you do MoT tests You know when the car needs replacing **Proves** that you **remember**

Pick one of your reasons and start writing the letter, but leave space to add more content. Deal with layout, recipient's name, date and sign off. The content requires a little more planning.

You should now have a letter that looks good, if rather meaningless; a good reminder perhaps that without a specific, clear reason, a letter, however well presented, will go straight into the bin. Think back to the opening chapter of this book and the concept that content should focus on the things you want the reader to **know**, **think** and **do**. Decide what these might be for your letter, then write the content of the letter, dealing with each of these three in turn.

Here's an example using the first reason for writing suggested above.

Dear Saleem

Now that you have been driving your new **Audi A4** for **three** months, I wanted to make sure you are enjoying life with your new car. It is, after all, only when you really get to know a new car, that you really appreciate its finer points. Do your **children** enjoy the ride in the back?

To help me tell more people about the comfort, economy, safety and tremendous value for money that Audi delivers, I'd be grateful if you would complete and return the enclosed short questionnaire. If you return it within two weeks, as a token of our gratitude for your honest feedback, we will give you a voucher worth £25, redeemable against the cost of your car's **first** service.

I look forward to hearing from you soon.

The example letter uses enough information that is personal to the reader (shown in bold type) for him to believe that he is the only recipient. This shows the value of maintaining a good customer database that contains more than just names and

addresses! Also guaranteed to boost response is an incentive to reply by a certain date. This is a vital ploy, as urgency always creates impact. The incentive offered is also in effect costing very little, particularly if the driver would not have chosen your garage for his next service. Remember the golden rule of marketing: that it is always better to sell more to existing customers than to find new customers.

Consumer or business to business

If you actually were a car dealer, you'd be far more likely to send letters than emails. This is because:

- Postal addresses usually change less frequently than email addresses
- Older people may not check their email very often
- People at home often find letters less intrusive than email

At work, however, even if the person you are targeting has moved on, someone will probably still open the email and read the message.

Databases

You will have seen from the example that the more you can tailor your letter to link with the reader, the more personal it will seem. This is perhaps not surprising. Consider, though, how many letters you receive that demonstrate clearly how little the writer has bothered to find out about you. Does anyone actually like being addressed as 'Dear Sir or Madam'?

Before getting too involved in this section, you might like to visit www.dataprotection.gov.uk to see how the legislation created in the UK to give people access to data about them might affect you. Do not be put off by regulation, the site will outline for you what constitutes good practice, and compliance with it will not inhibit effective marketing in the ways encouraged by this book. Also, you should explore some of the specialist 'contact management' software packages that exist. Where they differ from standard databases is that they can give you prompts. In other words, you can record when you next need to contact someone and why, and the software will remind you each day or week to do just that. This may seem unimportant if you only have a few customers or contacts. Remember, though, that to form a close and effective relationship with your contacts, you need to know as much about them as possible and let them know that you know too!

> Always be sure to have your customers' written consent to keep their information and send them offers. Use a customer satisfaction form to collect data and confirm permission.

Here are some examples of data you might choose to record and refer to in your written communication.

Information	Enables you to
Date of birth	Send a card (with product message) on their birthday Offer age-related products (credit cards at 18, etc)
Interests	Introduce contacts with shared interests Theme mailshots for groups of contacts
Company year end	Offer capital equipment at an appropriate time
Partner's name	Involve both (clearly) in the business idea suggested Invite both to events (partners often are involved in smaller businesses or work for one you've yet to reach with your marketing)
Product usage	Offer replenishment stock before a need is identified Develop planned (rather than emergency) maintenance

Practise writing paragraphs to go into your sales letters that contain some of this information. It will help you to appreciate how valuable it is, both in terms of relevance of message and in making it personal. Of course, you need to recognize that different situations demand different levels of communication 'intimacy'.

Here are some examples, one appropriate, the other not.

> Dear Tom, now that you are 18 you no longer have to rely on your parents' credit cards for making those online purchases. You can apply for your own card, which means that your purchases will not appear on their statement!
>
> Dear Mr George, having reached the age of majority, you are deemed capable of managing debt and, with this in mind, we are delighted to enclose for you an application form for our credit card.

If you had just turned 18, which do you feel would appeal more?

In writing letters to market your product or service, it is equally important to pitch your language at the age and situation of the reader. One letter will not 'fit all' and the more you can use technology to create an effective and accurate record of your prospects, the more personal your letter will appear when they read it.

Fax

The first edition of this book, written in 2002, described how and why you might use a fax. Today, you are unlikely to ever use a fax machine, except perhaps when sending signed documents or letters to very remote locations where internet access is limited.

A few top email tips

When writing an email, always remember that the recipient may view it on their computer in an office, on a laptop on the move or, increasingly, on their phone. It makes sense therefore to always:

- keep the message short and to the point
- seek a response – ask your recipient to 'click and reply'
- write in the first person (that is, 'I want to tell you about ...'
- avoid lurid backgrounds and 'comic' fonts. Refer back to Monday's chapter for ideas
- include your phone number so that phone users can call you immediately
- restrict subject lines to eight words. These will all be visible when the Inbox is viewed
- only use abbreviations and emoticons, e.g.;-) with those you know really well
- if you must include complex information, summarize and hyperlink to a webpage that can give more detail
- remember that some countries do not have fast broadband so avoid very large attachments

Summary

Today you have explored writing letters and emails. If you have completed the exercises, you'll have developed some new reasons for writing letters to those you want to influence. You will also have developed your letter writing style, adding a logical structure and flow. Formality versus familiarity has also been covered although much of this is for you to decide. If you are a young, informal person, you will write in a more chatty style than someone 30 years older.

Another point I hope you've grasped is that it really is OK to write as you would speak. Say it like it is and be yourself. Now put the book down and write to some people. Remember that even more important than doing it right is to do it at all!

SUNDAY

MONDAY

TUESDAY

WEDNESDAY

THURSDAY

FRIDAY

SATURDAY

Fact-check (answers at the back)

1. Invitations to prestigious events are best delivered:
   a) As emails ❑
   b) In a letter, perhaps with a leaflet enclosed ❑
   c) On a smart, gold-edged card ❑
   d) By phone ❑

2. Business information is usually best delivered:
   a) By printed memo ❑
   b) By email, with hyperlinks to relevant web references ❑
   c) By putting up a notice near the coffee machine ❑
   d) By letter so you know it's arrived ❑

3. Your emails will avoid the spam filters if you:
   a) Address each one personally to the right person ❑
   b) Send to lots of email addresses and hope one is correct ❑
   c) Buy a list from a broker ❑
   d) Avoid attachments ❑

4. Copywriting guru Drayton Bird says the most important thing is for your message to be:
   a) Interesting ❑
   b) Accurate ❑
   c) Illustrated ❑
   d) Personal ❑

5. The best reason for writing/emailing someone is to:
   a) Tell them about something new or time limited ❑
   b) Keep in touch ❑
   c) Get their feedback on what you're doing for them ❑
   d) Ask them why they're not buying from you ❑

6. Mailshots will be more effective if you:
   a) Pack the envelope with lots of bits of information ❑
   b) Start with a joke to cheer the readers up ❑
   c) Handwrite a personal PS to each letter ❑
   d) Just keep sending more and more ❑

7. Databases enable you to record information and then:
   a) Contact people at exactly the right time ❑
   b) Know that they've not died since you last wrote ❑
   c) Ask how their pet rabbit is getting along ❑
   d) Avoid writing to them too often ❑

8. Emails should always be short because:
   a) People are easily bored ❑
   b) The more you write the more you'll confuse people ❑
   c) Many will be read on a phone with a small screen ❑
   d) They're quicker to write ❑

9. Email subject lines should ideally:
   a) Explain everything in one long sentence ❑
   b) Be avoided as 'Re:' makes people curious ❑
   c) Be short and tempting ❑
   d) Contain a 'call to action' ❑

10. The best way to sign off a business email is with a simple:
    a) Regards ❑
    b) Love and kisses ❑
    c) Cheers ❑
    d) Till the next time ❑

WEDNESDAY

Making advertising work for you

Advertising is perhaps the most exciting form of copywriting. The space you purchase to deliver your message is usually expensive and must not be wasted. You do not know exactly who will read your words, so each one has to work really hard. Your writing must be clear, compelling and follow a logical sequence. You want your reader to follow your flow and get the message. Even more important is the need to stimulate responses. While many advertising experts talk about the importance of raising awareness, prompting action gives results you can measure. Today, you will:

Consider a range of types of advertisement

Explore the language of advertising

Practise writing advertising copy

Discover how to construct effective display advertisements

Consider unusual advertising opportunities, for example posters

Why do we advertise?

Advertising is used where your prospect cannot readily be identified and written to as an individual. It also has a role in building awareness and confidence in the product or service you are promoting. Raising awareness is particularly important with consumer products, where the manufacturer will advertise to create consumer desire. The retailer then supports this 'campaign' with in-store material (termed 'point-of-sale'), and the design of the packaging does the rest.

However, awareness-raising advertising is usually (and best) prepared by professional advertising agencies. This chapter will help you to prepare advertisements that you place to generate a direct response.

Here are some possible advertising opportunities that you might encounter.

Type	Opportunity
Classifieds	Selling a second-hand car
Recruitment	Finding new staff
Tenders	Seeking new suppliers
Directories	Listing your product/service next to those of your competitors
Exhibition catalogues	Encouraging visitors to your stand
Display advertising	Attracting new customers

You may be able to think of other advertising opportunities; some more are explored at the end of this chapter. It is fair to say, though, that the techniques you develop today will help you to prepare any kind of advertising copy. We will explore each in turn, for each demands different things from you, their writer.

The brief

Before you start writing, the one thing you must have is a clear brief. Until you know exactly what you want to say, why and how you want the reader to respond, writing good copy will be impossible. If you are writing the ad for yourself, you will probably know the full story of what, why, when, who and why. But if you are writing the copy for your boss or a colleague, you might need to help them give you a clear brief first.

This is what professional copywriters always do. It avoids confusion and potentially costly mistakes.

Here are some good questions you should always ask your client (or yourself) before you write a single word.

- **What** is the offer? What makes it better (for this audience) than the alternatives?
- **Who** is the target audience?
- **Which** attributes of the offer will appeal most? Is there evidence to support this?
- **Why** should the reader do something now? Urgency is vital to success.
- **When** will the ad appear or be read? At Christmas? Morning paper or evening paper?
- **Where** will it be read? At home, at work, commuting?
- **How** do you want your reader to respond? Phone, email, visit website, coupon?

Only when you are confident you have a clear brief can you expect to write an effective advertisement.

Writing style

All advertising copy has to paint a picture in the mind of the reader. Equally important is the need for brevity. In many ways, advertising is a good example of where 'less equals more'. In other words, the reader should be encouraged to use their imagination. You must not try to tell them too much. Remember also that good advertising copy flouts many of the rules you might have been taught about English grammar. You are writing for results, not an English exam!

Here are some examples that show how words can paint pictures.

What it is	How you describe it
Your wife's car needs replacing now a baby is on the way	Pregnancy forces sale of much loved 2009 Fiesta
The cat has just had kittens – again!	Fluffy, friendly kittens seek new homes
You need to recruit someone to clean lorries used to collect abattoir waste	If you've got the stamina, we've got the guts! Determined truck cleaner needed
You are a window cleaner	Want a brighter outlook? Let me make your windows sparkle

Note how powerful the example is that uses the word 'guts'. This is called a homonym and is where one word has two meanings. Both meanings are relevant to the line of copy, making it particularly memorable. This, along with the techniques of alliteration, simile and homophone described in Sunday's chapter, are all really good ways of making advertising copy stand out.

Now think of some advertising opportunities you might encounter and build a similar table. Try to include some from your home life and some that relate to work. The techniques are the same, but you will find them quite different to write.

Classified ads

Many of the examples given above apply well to classified advertising. This is where your ad appears in a column, on a page, under the publisher's classification. So you might be selling a car, and will have your car listed among everyone else's. In these situations, it is best to follow the convention used by the publication. For example, if it lists the cars alphabetically by make, you need to start your copy with the make of car, then move into some creative text.

There are different types of classified ad.

Lineage	All ads are printed in columns with each new ad starting on a separate line. The first few words are usually printed bold
Semi-display	As above, but usually with a line between ads, creating a little more space and a lot more impact
Display	As above, but with the words printed in a box
Colour	Sometimes colour can be used, usually a tint behind the ad. This invariably costs more

Classifieds are a good place to start writing advertising copy because they tend to be small, are often sold by the word and are very direct. These, however, are not reasons for them not being creative. The words need to fall into a clearly defined sequence.

What are you selling?	A description of the item. Follow the style of publication
Why should I buy it?	Further descriptive text that 'sells'
Where are you?	Important if you want buyers to visit you
How much?	What is the asking price and is it negotiable
How do I contact you?	Phone number, email address and website

Now assume that your company has just invested in some new office furniture and you want to sell the old desks. They are serviceable and clean but rather old. Your research tells you that they are probably only worth £50 each. Your company has a van, so you could deliver them.

Here are two possible ads. Which would you be most likely to respond to?

> **OFFICE DESKS** Clean and undamaged, choice of 10 modern double pedestal desks at our Wimbledon office. £50 + VAT each. Tel: 020 8123 4567 during office hours.
>
> **OFFICE DESKS** Office refit makes 10 good desks redundant. Perfect for a new business. £50 + VAT each. Can deliver. Wimbledon. Tel: 020 8123 4567 (9–5)

The second ad contains two fewer words, yet says so much more. Giving the reason for the sale, a 'refit', suggests that the sale is not prompted solely because the desks are tatty. It also helps to tell the reader who you think the desks will suit best. In this case, a business start-up where money is likely to be tight and appearance is important.

Now it's your turn to write some classified ads. Try to write, in fewer than 30 words, ads for:

- used wooden pallets
- 500 rolls of parcel tape
- a vacuum cleaner

Try also to bear in mind the likely context within which your ad will be read.

Recruitment

Have you noticed how, even in a time of slow economic growth, all the job ads you see are for people to join 'dynamic, fast-growing' businesses? Not everyone wants to work for this type of business, and if yours is a 'lifestyle' business, then say so in your ads. Recruitment advertising is rather like the 'lonely hearts' column. You want to find people you can get along with, not just people who can do the job.

Recruitment advertising is also the home of more copywriting clichés than even an estate agent's particulars. Take a look at your newspaper's jobs section; take a nice big display ad placed by a national firm. Now highlight all of those clichés and see what you're left with. The clichés mean nothing, the rest is what counts. Avoid at all costs phrases such as 'fast-growing' and 'rapidly changing', and never make a job out to be more than it really is. People respect honesty, and misrepresentation only leads to disappointment, either at interview or, worse, after a few weeks in the job.

Recruitment ads tend to be either classified or display, depending on the salary offered or the level of seniority. It's also true to say that more senior roles tend to be advertised nationally, with lesser roles advertised in local papers.

Here are two examples of ads for an office cleaner. Which appeals more to you? It appears in a section advertising part-time jobs.

> **Cleaner** required for busy restaurant. Hours flexible but must fit with opening times. 18 hours per week. £7.50 per hour. Call Luigi on 020 8789 6543
>
> **Cleaner** Delight our diners by keeping our busy restaurant spotless. 18 hours a week at times to suit us both. £135 per week. Call Luigi on 020 8789 6543

Can you see how the second one is more appealing? It shows that Luigi values what his cleaner does. He is willing to negotiate on hours, and the weekly pay sounds more attractive than the hourly rate. Both ads describe the restaurant as 'busy'. This is important because it reassures people that the job will last. A quiet restaurant may be easier to clean, but may find it difficult to afford a cleaner unless trade picks up.

Now you can try to write some recruitment classifieds. Think of a really good job, and a really awful one and write ads for both. Again, try to keep to about 30 words each.

With display recruitment advertising, there is a lot more scope for creativity, but beware. You can make an ad so creative that the original meaning is lost. In a good display recruitment ad you should have:

- Job title – describes exactly what the job is
- Rewards package – like it or not, if you don't mention a salary, people won't apply. Show a salary range
- What's involved – the kinds of duties that need to be done. Is travel involved? Is it a customer-facing role?
- Why you're recruiting – is it a new job, or a vacancy created by promotion or retirement?
- How to find out more – encourage people to visit your website to find out all about your organization. It's cheaper than trying to put it all in the ad. Also, include your logo where possible
- How to apply – do you just want people to write or email? An invitation to phone for an informal chat can be a great benefit to both parties
- What's so special? – always try to include something special that adds appeal. This could be funded training, subsidized travel, free health insurance or simply the fact that your organization has won awards for employee care

Now let's look at an example:

SALES MANAGER – USED CARS

Basic £30,000 pa + open-ended commission structure

Do you have the enthusiasm, drive and determination to lead our team of talented car sales professionals? If so, you will relish the challenge of building our turnover and sharing our profits. This new appointment is prompted by the recent completion of our used car showroom next to the city football ground.

We can offer you a competitive package, budget responsibility and full marketing support.

For an informal chat, call our MD Steve Smith on 01234 456789 or email him on ss@classymotors.co.uk

---

Can you see how the ad is full of positive news? This is a new job, at a new showroom next door to a place where lots of used car buyers regularly congregate. There is a team to manage, a budget as well and the package is open ended. Also, as many potential candidates will already be working for local rivals, they are invited to 'phone for an informal chat'. If the job was for, say, an accountant, then it would be more appropriate to ask for a written application supported by references. Can you see how you need to vary the style according to the role and organization? Now write a job ad for your own role; it's the one you know best. When you've finished, see how it resembles the reality of what you do at work.

Directories

Perhaps the most common directory is the 'Yellow Pages', one of the few still popular in both print and online versions. Here, as with other forms of advertising, you have to provide your copy with no knowledge of what will appear around it. Many advertisers, encouraged by the sales representative, book large expensive ads in the hope of catching more customers' eyes than the smaller ads of their rivals. In fact, it is often words or images that leap off the page, rather than the size of the ad, that make the difference.

Directory ads can be very expensive and people often buy them because they feel that they 'should' be in there. Here are a few techniques that will make your directory ads more effective.

Feature	Example
Make the headline personal	*Our* printer accessories last *you* years
Link to your website. It will be updated more often than the directory	Visit www.bumperdeals.co.uk for this week's special offer
Encourage enquiries, as well as orders (you will get more calls and more sales!)	Ring for your FREE copy of our guide to home improvements
Offer several ways to respond	Ring, fax, email, write or call in...

Exhibition catalogues

The joy of an exhibition catalogue is that you know that people will read it, either at the exhibition or when they get back to the office. While you are in effect buying a directory ad and should write it accordingly, you do have the opportunity to link the ad to your stand. For example:

● 'Bring this ad to our stand and we'll give you a free cup of coffee'
● 'Ring us and quote "ExEx12" and we will pack a free gift with your first order'
● 'Visit our stand, under the pink balloons, and we'll give you a balloon to take home for your kids'

Picture your stand, or the staff on it, in the ad. The curious will come and look to see if they're the same!

Display ads

So far, we have focused on low cost advertising, largely because this is where you are most likely to be asked to write advertising copy. However, some of the most successful display advertising campaigns have been developed by those working within the organization. Advertising agencies can add value in many ways, but it is always good to have some strong ideas of your own before delegating this important aspect of your marketing.

If you check back to the section of Monday's chapter that covers how the eye scans a page, you will appreciate why most ads have a picture at the top, a headline below and the descriptive text, called body copy, underneath. The reply coupon, phone number, voucher or other 'call to action' is usually at the bottom right. This is where the eye 'instinctively' ends its journey through your ad.

There are countless excellent books that describe, analyse and teach the art of advertising copywriting. Here, you are encouraged to just consider the basics.

Let us assume then that you have decided to place a series of display ads for your company's IT training courses. You have agreed the brief with your colleagues and want to attract 100 people to join ten half-day sessions that you have called 'The internet for beginners'. You particularly want to attract older people, who might be looking for income to top-up their pensions by trading on eBay, or who simply want to keep in touch with their families. This is what the ad could look like:

Note how the bravery theme keeps coming up in the text. Also the way the headline, body copy and image are linked. People will phone to ask for a leaflet, providing you with the opportunity to sell them a place. The ad is also explicit in setting out what the cost is and what is included. Most people will feel reassured by this. Again, give no price and they will not ring to ask in case it is too expensive.

To reinforce your skills at writing display ads, find some in a magazine or trade journal and see how they follow the principles described in this book. Then, taking one that appeals to you, try to rewrite it and make it better. Then, write an ad for your organization using the style of the ad you've been working on. Finally, show the work to a trusted colleague or perhaps your partner at home. Ask for constructive feedback. Do they get the message you are trying to convey?

Unusual advertising

Advertising can be fun, especially if your product or service lends itself to advertising in unusual locations. Here are a few examples to stimulate your imagination:

Location	Headline	Product
Back of a bus	'Ever wished your car had more poke?'	High performance cars
Above a urinal	'Can we lend you a hand?'	Temping agency offering factory staff
Roadside hoarding	'No one queues on our network'	Telecoms provider
Restaurant bill	'Need a taxi?'	Minicab firm
Bus (upstairs)	'Enjoy more of a view?'	Holidays
In a lift	'Feeling hot?'	Deodorant

Summary

Today, you have explored advertising and now have a better understanding of how to write with the clarity and focus needed in this challenging, yet creative environment. You have also practised writing copy for a variety of ads and have come to realize that with advertising, less really can deliver more. This chapter has also provided a welcome opportunity to put into practice much of what has been covered in the earlier chapters, for it is in advertising that typography and photography really come into their own.

You should now feel confident to move on and consider how else you can improve your organization's image and marketing through the expert use of your pen.

SUNDAY

MONDAY

TUESDAY

WEDNESDAY

THURSDAY

FRIDAY

SATURDAY

Fact-check (answers at the back)

1. You only know your advertising works when:
   a) You hear people talking about your ad in the street ❏
   b) Your competitors start copying you ❏
   c) You provoke a reader response ❏
   d) Your agency wins a creative advertising award ❏

2. The first thing you should write before planning some advertising is:
   a) The headline ❏
   b) Some copy ❏
   c) A brief ❏
   d) Your weekend shopping list ❏

3. Good advertising copy:
   a) Paints a vivid picture ❏
   b) Highlights the facts, flaws and all ❏
   c) Uses long sentences ❏
   d) Fills the ad ❏

4. More important than saying what it is, say:
   a) Why you're advertising it ❏
   b) Who you want the reader to be ❏
   c) Where you make the product ❏
   d) What it does – the benefits ❏

5. The first thing you look at when planning a classified ads is:
   a) Previous ads placed by your organization ❏
   b) Ads you've responded to yourself ❏
   c) The ceiling in search of inspiration ❏
   d) Some recent ads from the same section of the same paper ❏

6. Many recruiters overlook the importance of showing:
   a) The basic duties of the job ❏
   b) The pay ❏
   c) Where the job will be based ❏
   d) That the job is valued and important to the organization ❏

7. The most important word to use in an ad is:
   a) You ❏
   b) Me ❏
   c) We ❏
   d) I ❏

8. In display advertising the picture and text should:
   a) Work together to convey a clear message ❏
   b) Contradict each other to make the reader think ❏
   c) Each cover half of the space ❏
   d) Use the same predominant colours ❏

9. Advertising on the back of a bus means:
   a) Your message gets obliterated by exhaust fumes ❏
   b) You can tailor your text to the driver of the following car ❏
   c) You'll always save money over roadside hoardings ❏
   d) Bus passengers will be sure to spot your ad ❏

10. Writing good advertising copy should be:
    a) Hard work ❏
    b) Boring ❏
    c) Challenging ❏
    d) Fun ❏

69

THURSDAY

Communicating clearly with the media

SUNDAY

MONDAY

TUESDAY

WEDNESDAY

THURSDAY

FRIDAY

SATURDAY

People tend to believe what they are told by the media. It is simply more believable than the messages delivered by advertising and direct mail. There is a skill to generating effective press coverage. Today, you will develop that skill and practise the art of managing media relations. You will see that there is much more to it than just badgering journalists to write your story. Sometimes we are lucky and our story is very newsworthy in its own right, but in business that is rarely the case.

Today you will:

Learn how to build good relationships with journalists

Find out how material is selected for publication

Practise writing news releases

Discover the value of becoming a media commentator. Recognize that bad news needs releasing as well as good

How do journalists work?

Contrary to what you might have been led to believe, journalism today is a tough job. It's much more than a life of leisurely writing punctuated by expensive lunches provided by PR agencies. Harsh commercial pressures on media owners mean that costs have been trimmed to the extent where on all but the most popular titles, journalists have little time to go out and seek stories. They have to rely on the news coming to them. Most newspapers for example subscribe to news feed services such as Reuters and the Press Association, which provide a constant flow of national and international news, accompanied by pictures, for the journalists and editors to buy. Much of the manpower is focused on researching and writing stories that are of interest to the target reader but which, without journalistic effort, would not make it to the newsroom. Examples are crime, politics and health.

Your opportunity is clear. If you operate in a business environment, you will see that in many instances the newspapers, journals and magazines are relying on you to tell them what's going on. Before moving on to techniques, though, it is important to recognize that the media is extensive and varied and not all publications come readily to mind. Here are some types of publication together with their benefits to you as a publicist.

Media type	Benefits
Community publications such as parish magazines	Usually produced by amateurs and desperate for material. Perfect for local retail businesses
Professional network newsletters	Again, usually produced by amateurs and usually eager to accept copy that adds to their members' professional development. (Remember too to offer yourself as a speaker to these networks.)
Local weekly newspapers	Frequently will give free editorial to advertisers, so always ask. If free circulation (not paid for), they often welcome product-linked competitions as these allow them to demonstrate that people actually read the newspaper!

Media type	Benefits
Regional dailies	Usually under severe pressure from nationals and keen to print positive local stories. Also, usually reluctant to print damaging or negative stories that can jeopardize advertising revenue
Local radio/TV	Both the BBC and independent stations are usually happy to publicize good stories. You can also find yourself invited for a live interview
Specialist magazines	A quick online search will reveal that there is a magazine for every conceivable consumer or business interest. If you sell to a specialist sector, these titles can be your lifeline
Business journals	Behave in the same way as the regional newspapers
National daily newspapers	Have big editorial teams and are deluged with news releases. You need to be practised or lucky to get results here. Beware of damaging backfires
National Sunday newspapers	Behave like the national dailies, except that they have large teams researching and writing features (interesting, but not news). They also frequently contract out sections to independent writers, who are easier to influence
Mass market magazines	Behave like national Sundays – but focus on their niche
National TV	Similar to local radio/TV; seek out the production companies
Media websites	All of the above will have news websites. Some will be more widely read than the print edition. Increasingly, online and downloadable editions are replacing traditional print editions

You can see that there is a complex array of media to choose from. As a rule, it always makes sense to target those that:

● share your target audience (interests, industry, geography)
● carry advertising from organizations in your sector (particularly your competitors!)
● you know your existing customers read, trust and enjoy
● you read regularly yourself because they inform you

Here, you will stand a better chance of being heard. It is also easier to build a relationship with writers on specialist or regional titles, simply because you both know that there is more to be gained. National journalists, by the very nature of their publications, have to move quickly, grab the story, exploit it and move on. They are rarely interested in follow-up stories and may appear rude and abrupt. In fact, they are only doing what is actually a very challenging and stressful job.

How are news releases selected for publication?

Before moving on to write your release, it is important to see how things are in a busy editorial office. Then you can appreciate why it is important to work in a way that makes the lives of journalists easier.

Journalists are driven by deadlines. A daily newspaper for example will have several deadlines a day. Features writers have much longer deadlines, so consequently work further ahead than their news colleagues.Weekly and monthly titles will have a mixture of features that are not time-critical and stories that are current at the time of publication. Lastly, most publications have a constantly changing pool of 'filler' pieces that can be dropped in at the last minute if, for example, a story scheduled for publication is stopped by the courts (by an injunction) or, less glamorously, if an advertiser misses a copy deadline and there's suddenly a space to fill.

To succeed in getting your news published you have to recognize how an editorial team works and present your story at the most appropriate time. For example, if you are approaching a daily paper about:

Event	Procedure
Celebrity visit to your premises / Photogenic event (e.g. chimney demolition)	Email the release two days before the event Include biography of celebrity/information One day before – ring to follow up At 9.30 a.m. on the day – ring again
Major contract win/jobs created	Email release straight away Follow up the next day
Interesting (but not time-sensitive story)	Send in with a good photo and wait!
Disaster	Prepare your statement and ring the editor Listen first, and be prepared to say 'I'll check that out and ring you back' (then do it!)

Writing a release

There is a clearly defined sequence you must follow when putting together a news release. We will deal with each of these in turn.

Photographs

Funnily enough, the most desirable feature of a good press release is a professionally taken, appropriate photograph. Newspapers are always short of good shots and those that accompany your release will boost your chances of exposure.
   Photographs should:

- create a visual metaphor, e.g. an interesting shot of people with the product linked to the headline of the release
- avoid visual clichés, e.g. handshakes, giant cheques or large groups of people
- not overtly promote your brand, i.e. not look like an advertisement
- catch the eye, i.e. be innovative, yet acceptable to the paper

   So, the first thing you need when writing your release is a good picture. Often, thinking of the picture will give you a lead into the headline and story you want to write.

Headlines

Headlines should be short (up to ten words), attention grabbing and clearly linked to your picture. Use the techniques already covered to make the line punchy and memorable. Homophones, homonyms and alliteration are particularly powerful when used in headlines. For example:

> 'Major contract makes **plane** sailing (homophone) – joinery business wins big order
>
> 'Cash crisis **dogs** cats' home' (homonym) – an appeal for funds
>
> 'Mouse mat moves millions' (alliteration) – mouse-mat company's new product

Headlines should also use the style of language that your target reader will be most comfortable with. In a trade journal, for example, your headline can be quite specific and technical. It needs only to be understood by a knowledgeable journalist and the expert reader. In the consumer press, however, jargon and acronyms (e.g. IIP) should be avoided. Better to state the name in full (e.g. Investors in People).

Practise writing some headlines yourself. Here are three stories.

Story	Photograph
City mayor welcomes first 'budget airline' service to local airport	Mayor in official garb, in front of plane, holding a £20 note and a passport
Leading research chemist becomes non-executive director of your company	Scientist in white coat with can of your product over a Bunsen burner
Famous chat-show hostess opens social housing development	The famous person hugging an old lady in the doorway of her new home

The first paragraph

After the headline, this is the most important section. Many journalists will read no further and will take the headline and the content of your first paragraph to create a 20–40 word caption for the picture. Or they will use the same words without a picture as a 'nib' (news in brief). Nibs are the columns of news snippets that often run down one side of the page. Therefore, your first paragraph has to summarize all that you want to say. Here is an example:

> # Handy to shake Essex entrepreneurs
>
> Colchester-based ABC Training will welcome business guru Charles Handy as guest speaker at its 'enterprise conference' taking place on 3rd March at 6pm. Handy will be speaking about the growth of social enterprise. Tickets cost £25 and can be booked by ringing 01206 123456

You can see that the paragraph contains the location, date, time, host, speaker, ticket price and a contact number. Everything, in fact, that is needed for the reader to make contact with you.

Subsequent paragraphs

The second paragraph should support and expand on the first. Remember, this paragraph may get cut or missed out altogether, so it has to really add value. One of the best ways to do this is to include a quote. Quotes are important because they do not often get edited. They are either reproduced in their entirety or simply discarded. In the example above, a quote by Charles Handy would almost certainly be used; a quote by the CEO of ABC Training, only possibly; and one by someone else, probably not at all. Because quotes are printed as quotes, it is essential to have the written permission of the person you are quoting to include the quote in your news release. If you don't, they can sue you. Here's a possible second paragraph for our release.

> 'The similarities between Handy's experience and Colchester's business base is amazing,' commented Bill Hook, CEO of ABC Training. 'Many of our businesses have been started by exiles from corporate life, reinventing themselves as what Handy would call "fleas".'

You can see that the second paragraph consists of a quote by the CEO. Handy, we can surmise, chose not to offer a quote for publication. The quote reinforces the relevance of the event in the reader's mind. It seeks to link the speaker's topic with Colchester.

A third paragraph might contain further evidence supporting the significance of the event. It might quote government statistics on Colchester's business population and the researched barriers to their greater success. These could then be linked with more information about the speaker's presentation.

Lastly, a press release needs to have a clear end (it needs to say just that) and be followed by information about the accompanying photo, together with contact details so that the journalist can find out more if they wish. Here is an example of how a release might end. Having sent in your release, it is important to be easily contactable. Many releases are considered, then binned because the journalist cannot get answers to questions when they need them.

> ... Colchester's businesses are predominantly run by men in their 40s.
>
> **ENDS**
>
> Picture shows, left to right, Bill Hook, CEO ABC Training, Charles Handy, Taff Dell, Founder of SX Computers, Colchester – at ABC Training's Station Road premises
>
> For further information:
>
> Bill Hook, Tel. 01206 123456 Mob. 01712 345678
> bill@abctraining.co.uk

Becoming a commentator

Newspapers, particularly local and regional titles, constantly seek to put a local slant on national and international stories. You can help them to achieve this and gain valuable publicity for your business at the same time. This is what you have to do:

Spot stories that are relevant to your organization	'Fiasco at Tax Office as 10% of tax returns submitted on last day'
Identify your opportunity to put your own 'spin' on the story	You are proactive and all of your clients' returns were sent in two weeks ago
Contact relevant local/ journalist	'It's as much the accountant's fault for being passive and not helping their clients meet the deadline. We do [X, Y, Z] and all of ours were in two weeks ago.
Journalist runs follow up story the next morning	You are quoted as a responsible accountant who blames less professional firms for fiasco
Journalist writing piece on similar subject in future	Rings you for a comment, which gets you, and your firm's name, in the paper

As a good copywriter, you will be able to translate the national headlines into stories that you can submit as comments. It is all down to creative thinking and seeing what could be. Try to write 100-word comments that can be emailed to your local newspaper or business magazine on the following topics.

- Your company has won an award
- Your organization has partnered with a charity to encourage staff volunteering

Now consider the possibilities offered by the following:

You are	National story
Shoe retailer	'Fashion shoes can deform children's feet'
Coach operator	'Tunnel work will close main rail-line for two weeks'
Conveyancer	'Searches failed to spot planned asylum seekers' camp'
Hospital administrator	'Patient left on trolley for 24 hours in casualty'

Here's an example to help you, based on the final story in the list above. Note how the quote, which will not be changed, forms the largest part of the comment.

> Commenting on the saga of Jack Dawe, the pensioner left on a trolley for 24 hours at London Central Hospital, Bill Sykes, Administrator at Anytown General said, "However busy our casualty department gets, we have the procedures in place to make sure that this could never happen here. Every patient is checked in on arrival and an automatic system of 'pager-prompts' make sure that they are never overlooked, however busy we are." Mr Sykes went on to tell us that Anytown General regularly stages major disaster exercises which tests their system to the limits of feasibility. One of the key measures of success for these exercises is the extent to which other emergency admissions are delayed by the rush as disaster survivors are brought in.

The first part of the comment is what you might have written. The second part results from a conversation with the journalist. It is always good to have some bullet points noted down on what you want to say before phoning the media.

Blogs

Most publications also welcome regular blogs from qualified commentators. These can be a powerful way of spreading your message. A good blog on an existing media website should:

● be topical, short and make a clear point to provoke comment
● express an opinion, not promote your business
● end with your name and what you do
● link to your website

Dealing with the unexpected

However staid your organization, there is always the chance that it will hit the headlines. Accidents, fires, industrial tribunals, legal battles and employee misdemeanours can all attract unwelcome publicity. The worst thing that anyone can do in this situation is to say 'no comment'. In print this is likely to look like an admission of failure. When unexpected things happen, you should prepare a statement. You often see these read out by solicitors on TV news broadcasts, standing outside a court. A statement is very different from a press release. It will often be quoted verbatim by the media and should (if the event is serious enough) be checked over by your own solicitor before distribution.

Statements are usually:

- **factual,** and explicit in the way they tell your version of the story
- **third person** – the organization is 'speaking', so it's usually 'Company X believes that ...'
- **straight** – no humour, or scope for anyone to take offence

Here's an example. You are a school headteacher and your caretaker has just been arrested for downloading indecent material onto his computer. Your statement might read:

> 'Mr Green is an excellent caretaker and has been with us for twenty years. The alleged offence took place when he was at home, using his own personal computer. The governing body has, however, decided to suspend him on full pay pending the outcome of police investigations. We hope that we will soon be able to reinstate him and wish to reassure parents that we have absolutely no evidence that his behaviour while at school has ever given cause for concern.'

Key points to note when writing a statement are:

- Start with a positive – this reassures people and also shows you are unbiased
- Explain the facts – in our example, the alleged offence took place at home
- Explain your actions – what has been done and why
- Confirm your findings – what have you found out that will reassure readers?

Summary

Today, you have found out how journalists operate and why they behave the way they do. They do a difficult job and have to please their readers, editors, publishers and advertisers as well as you. You have also found out how a good picture can boost a news release's chances of publication.

Your copywriting skills have been developed as you have practised writing news releases. You have prepared comments that you might send to gain publicity through association with existing, topical stories. Finally, you have gained an appreciation of the importance of issuing a statement rather than remaining silent when disaster strikes.

Just before you leave this aspect of copywriting, it is perhaps worth recognizing the value of email in communicating with the media. Whereas once, news releases were posted to publications, now increasingly they are emailed, with digital photos (ideally saved in JPEG format and attached alongside the release). This means that if you are quick, you can have your comment on the morning's big story in the journalist's inbox before he arrives at work. This speed of response benefits both you, as the promoter, and the paper, for it enables printed media to, in some ways, keep up with more spontaneous media such as radio.

SUNDAY

MONDAY

TUESDAY

WEDNESDAY

THURSDAY

FRIDAY

SATURDAY

Fact-check (answers at the back)

1. The best way to publicize your organization and what you do is:
   a) To buy lots of last-minute discounted advertising ❑
   b) To use the best advertising agency money can buy ❑
   c) To put advertising on all your vehicles ❑
   d) To have good things written about you in the press ❑

2. Generating media publicity is becoming easier because:
   a) Most journalists have a drink problem and no longer write ❑
   b) There are fewer journalists and a growing demand for content ❑
   c) Rising fuel costs prevent journalists going out to cover stories ❑
   d) The trend away from print to web means less demand for content ❑

3. National journalists move:
   a) Quickly because stories have a very short life ❑
   b) Slowly because tonight's TV contains tomorrow's papers' news ❑
   c) Rarely because they eat too much ❑
   d) Mountains to unearth every angle on a story ❑

4. The best publications to offer your news stories to are:
   a) Those you enjoy reading yourself ❑
   b) Those read in business sectors where you are weak ❑
   c) Those read in business sectors where you are strong ❑
   d) Those read by people like you ❑

5. The best time to contact journalists about an event is:
   a) A week before ❑
   b) Two days before ❑
   c) On the day ❑
   d) Two days later ❑

6. Good photos really boost your chances of getting published if they:
   a) Show two people shaking hands in front of your office ❑
   b) Provide an eye-catching visual metaphor for the story ❑
   c) Have your company or brand name prominently displayed ❑
   d) Were taken on the spur of the moment with your phone ❑

7. Your news release has to capture all the relevant information:
   a) Over no more than three pages of A4 ❑
   b) In the headline ❑
   c) In the first paragraph ❑
   d) In an accompanying explanatory leaflet ❑

8. When you send in a news release it's important to:
a) Provide a mobile phone number so the journalist can contact you 24/7 ❑
b) Send it to every journalist on the paper whose email address you have ❑
c) Use desktop publishing to make it look as if it's already in the paper ❑
d) Phone to follow up within an hour ❑

9. The best way to build your profile in the media is to:
a) Buy journalists expensive lunches ❑
b) Send them short, pithy comments they can use the moment a relevant story breaks ❑

c) Ring them every week to get to know them better ❑
d) Send them gifts at the end of the year ❑

10. Blogs are really useful, but only if you:
a) Make them long and comprehensive ❑
b) Create your own blog site and post them there ❑
c) Invite other people to write them for you ❑
d) Post them on websites visited by lots of those you want to influence ❑

SUNDAY

MONDAY

TUESDAY

WEDNESDAY

THURSDAY

FRIDAY

SATURDAY

FRIDAY

Preparing promotional print

Promotional print brings together many of the copywriting, typographical and visual skills you have developed as you've worked through the book. Only advertising offers similar creative opportunities. Increasingly, promotional fliers and leaflets are distributed electronically, in PDF format.

Printed material remains important, particularly in consumer markets. For the smaller organization this is produced in-house, using desktop publishing software. Large brochures and catalogues are usually professionally produced, although you will still need to provide a brief.

Far and away the most common scenario is where a graphic designer, either freelance or with a small agency, is hired to create the visual aspects of your print. It is left to you as the client, however, to prepare the words.

Today, you will:

Pick up some tips on choosing promotional print

Gain an understanding of how the print business works

Practise writing brochure copy

Appreciate the value of covering letters, then practise writing one

Discover how you can make it easy for people to respond

The basics

Producing promotional print is always a compromise. In an ideal world, you would tailor each copy to the needs and interests of the person you are sending it to. If you know who they are, you can do this using digital printing.

Most print, however, is placed in a rack and picked up by passers-by. You therefore have to generalize and make assumptions about your reader. Your copywriting has to capture and hold their attention. Ideally it also has to prompt them to do what the printed material encourages. Often, this is to make an enquiry or purchase.

Here are some examples to help you match your message to the right print medium.

Project	Printed solution
Invitations to a reception/ presentation	Gilt-edged cards
Internal document about training options	Desktop published and photocopied
External document about training courses	Simple colour printed leaflets
Annual report	Professionally designed colour brochure
Product launch	Full-colour mailshot with reply card
Corporate brochure	Professionally designed colour brochure

When buying printing services for leaflets and brochures, you need to remember a few simple facts about the printing process. These will help you to get the best value from your investment.

- How many pages? – most presses print four pages at a time, so multiples of four pages will always be the most cost effective
- What paper? – standard gloss, matt or silk art papers are always far cheaper than more specialist papers. It's cheaper to use special finishes than special paper

- Paper weight – weights, measured in grammes per square metre (gsm), are usually used as follows:
  - 80 gsm – copier
  - 90 gsm – letterhead
  - 115 gsm – lightweight leaflet (often A4 folded to fit standard DL size envelope)
  - 135 gsm – most brochures and leaflets
  - 200 gsm – brochure cover pages (if different from contents)
  - 350 gsm – folders and invitation cards, etc
- Special finishes
  - 'spot varnish' is a glossy finish applied to part of the page (e.g. over pictures)
  - 'lamination' is a glossy or matt finish often added to covers
- Quantity
  - use digital printers for runs of fewer than 500 copies
  - use litho printers for runs of over 500
- Pictures
  - never skimp on photography
  - never use digital images that are low resolution, i.e. less than 150 dots per inch (dpi)
- Providing artwork – for all but the simplest designs, ask your graphic designer to supply finished artwork as a digital file

Writing promotional copy

As you will rapidly discover, you can spend a lot of money on print and it is natural to be very proud of your brochures and the messages they contain. However, you must remember when writing your promotional copy that often brochures are filed away and referred to weeks, months and even years later. It is important, therefore, that the words work really hard and can manage on their own without you to interpret them. Here are a few golden rules:

- Make frequent use of the words **you** and **yours**. They build the reader relationship
- Avoid writing in the third person. Better to make the words a personal message

- Talk benefits, not features. Focus on what's important to the reader, not to you. (How often do you see photographs of factories and vans, rather than happy customers?)
- Use pictures to tell the story. Use captions and tables to make things clear
- Ask questions in the copy to focus the reader's thoughts where you want them

Here's an example of how you might choose to describe a public speaking training programme in a leaflet aimed at middle managers seeking to build their confidence:

Presentation skills for nervous speakers

This one-day course is designed to overcome the natural fears we all face when asked to speak to a group. Working alongside no more than nine other delegates, you will have the opportunity to discover why everyone finds public speaking daunting, then learn and practise techniques to overcome the fear. You will gain the confidence to make a short video-recorded presentation. You will receive individual support, feedback and tips as you develop your own speaking style.

The example shows exactly who the course is aimed at and implies that the provider recognizes your nervousness and will not take you too far out of your comfort zone. A small group of like-minded people, along with individual feedback, is reassuring. Would you sign up for this?

Now, in a similar way, practise describing something your organization provides its customers with. Create a block of around 70 words. Think too about what images might illustrate the benefits your reader will relate to. Often the best image will form a visual metaphor for the benefits you are trying to illustrate. For example, you might illustrate our public-speaking course with a pair of wrenching hands, rather than an image of a confident speaker at a lectern. People buy things that relate to where they are right now, as well as those

that hint at reaching their goal. In fact, showing the goal alone
can tend to make its attainment look virtually impossible. It's
good to show your reader that you understand where they're
starting from.

Benefits

It is worth pausing a while to consider benefits versus features.
Every aspect of your offer, when presented in promotional
print, should be described in terms of the value it offers to the
typical reader. Remember that people do not buy things, they
buy what things will do. Here are some examples:

Feature	Benefit
Company website	You can place your orders whenever you wish
Fleet of 10 vans	We deliver in your neighbourhood every day
Car with cruise control	Discover the joy of passing traffic cameras without worrying about your speed
First-class rail tickets	Non-standard people need non-standard accommodation; buy yourself space to think
Spectacle cleaning fluid	Let people see your eyes, not greasy thumbprints

Benefits are often emotionally derived and not linked at all to
the actual physical nature of the product. First-class carriages
tend to have fewer seats and thus more space. But space

alone is no incentive to buy. Space to think, however, flatters the reader by suggesting that their thoughts will be valuable and worth the extra investment. Practise writing benefit statements for the following:

- UHT long-life milk
- a smartphone
- courses that increase your typing speed

Stopping and starting

Your reader will scan the page and only pick up some of the words. They will then, if you are lucky, go back to the interesting bits to read some more. It is helpful therefore to have some techniques to hand that will encourage your reader to stop and think. And also some ways to direct them towards the next section most appropriate for them. A good way to get your reader to reflect on your words is to ask a rhetorical question: a question that is asked in order to make a statement and that does not expect an answer. Naturally, as you won't be there when the copy is read and the question asked, it has to be rhetorical. Here is an example:

> Ask yourself, when passing traffic speed cameras, how often you find yourself looking at your speedometer rather than the car in front? This is natural, but also potentially dangerous. This is because in your enthusiasm to avoid a speeding fine, you run the risk of colliding with the car in front should it stop suddenly. A good way to avoid both fines and accidents is to make sure that your car is fitted with cruise control.

You can also ask the reader to 'tell you' what they think. Of course, in reality they can't, but you can make them think of what they might say if they could. Building questions into your copy brings it alive and creates a conversation with the reader. Conversation is always more interesting than simply listening to speech. Questions involve the reader, and involved readers continue reading.

One way to direct the reader towards the most relevant section is to produce tables or use colour to provide signposts through the text for the reader. For example:

> 'What kind of dog do you have? If it is short haired, turn to the comb selection on the opposite page. If it has long hair, the products described below are more suitable.'

The conversational, directive style will help the reader find their way about. It will save them time and, by acknowledging that dogs have both short and long hair, demonstrates knowledge and understanding of the reader's situation.

Captions

You have already discovered why captions are important. They make it easy for the reader to understand why you have placed the picture on the brochure for them to see. For example, a photo showing the view of a dashboard and car windscreen could pose a question. Where do you look first? Or it could be a photo of a finger on the cruise control switch, with the caption 'Cruise control is simple and safe to use'. Avoid stating the obvious, unless the obvious is not going to be obvious to every reader. With technical brochures, for example, you often need to show people what the product looks like. In these cases, the caption needs to be explicit and descriptive. Sometimes, several captions are needed, each with an arrow pointing to the feature they describe.

Brochure flow

Rather like a sales letter, the information in your leaflet or brochure needs to follow a logical sequence. Unlike a sales letter, you have more space to work with and can provide a number of routes through your copy using the techniques already described. Part of the skill of a good graphic designer is to make it easy to follow a clear, visual route through your piece of print. Here, though, is a rough guide to how a brochure should be structured.

1 Front cover – instantly recognizable key benefit to reader
2 First section – explains what the product or service is and why it is of value
3 Middle section – offers examples, customer testimonials, alternatives
4 Rear section – specifications if needed
5 Every page – how to find out more, e.g. phone number and website address
6 Back cover – all contact details, and perhaps endorsing logos (e.g. ISO9001)

The covering letter

You have already come to appreciate that effective copy is personalized copy. That is, where you can create the illusion that the words have been written specifically with the individual reader in mind. By the very nature of the printing process, leaflets and brochures can be produced in vast quantities. How, then, can you personalize the message for each recipient? The answer of course is to write a covering letter. A number of techniques have already been described in this book, for example, the use of mail-merge and a good database to embed personal information in the letter. When a letter introduces an enclosed piece of print, you can go a little further and really make the reader feel you are writing to them alone. Here is an example extract from a letter that accompanies a coach holiday brochure sent to an existing customer.

> You will see from page 12 that we are once more returning to Blackpool, a destination I know you have visited with us before. This time, we have included a free night-time tour to see the famous winter lights. I hope this will tempt you to travel with us again in 2012.

Naturally, linking your bookings history with a mail-merge means that you can automatically adapt each letter according to the purchasing history of your customer. This, together with taking the time to hand sign each letter, really makes recipients read the brochure you've invested in producing.

Think about how you could personalize the covering letters you might send to people you are mailing with promotional material. Practise integrating specific information that will make the letter personal. Think too about how to make it easy to merge. Unless you are careful, you will find that some versions of your letter look odd. It is all too easy to become blasé when despatching lots of brochures and covering letters. You must always take care to ensure that when the envelope is opened, the communication is very personal to the reader. They will have the time to spot any errors you have made.

Here are a few more tips for writing covering letters.

- Bookmarks – when referring to a specific page (as in the example above), why not insert a Post-it™ note to mark the page? If every letter refers to the same page, the printer can insert the bookmarks for you
- Endorsements – it might carry more weight if the covering letter is from someone other than you. For example, if promoting an event with a leading speaker, ask the speaker to agree to the letter going out as if written by them. This can be a powerful delegate attractant
- Joint letters – often, professionals collaborate to run events and campaigns. If you are a solicitor working alongside an accountant, prepare a special letterhead with both logos and have it signed by both too. Unique combinations of familiar brands really catch a reader's eye
- Gimmicks – in the right situations, enclosing things such as a free pen or window sticker can add impact. Better still, link it to the message. For example, an explosives company could enclose a balloon and a pin, in case you want to make your own big bangs!
- Be natural – take your products' benefits to your customer. An egg producer might enclose a soft feather. A garden centre some seeds. A tourist attraction some pressed flowers, and so on

Provoking a response

Of course what makes all the effort worthwhile is the response. You're sending out material to tempt people to purchase and so every effort must be made to provoke an enquiry. Your copy needs to encourage readers to seek further information or indeed to place an order. Here are a few techniques to help you do this:

- Order form – include order forms with your brochure. Always send a new order form with the goods, plus an incentive to buy again
- Survey – a simple questionnaire asking your reader's views, plus offering to share the findings, will encourage response and give you valuable feedback. Good for capital goods which will not be ordered 'off the page'
- Incentive to refer – offer a discount on the first order if two additional prospects are provided for your database. Always use the referee's name when following up
- Keep writing – follow-up letters are invaluable and are proven to work
- Introduce deadlines – early-order discounts are a good way to provoke a response
- Offer choice – the more ways to order (phone, fax, web) and the longer the opening hours (always state them) the more you'll sell

Make a list of the things you want your readers to do. It might be to place an order, book a place on a programme or simply to ask for more information. Remember that it is always better to provide several small steps for your prospects to follow. Make it easy for them to move towards your desired outcome.

Now, think about your own organization. What are the steps you could ask your audience to take? How many are there? Write some paragraphs that seek commitment to each one. How does this compare with what you are currently doing? As you refine and test the process, you can monitor both the additional cost of more frequent communication and the return. Try, too, to make it fun.

SUNDAY MONDAY TUESDAY WEDNESDAY THURSDAY FRIDAY SATURDAY

Summary

Today, you have gained an insight into how brochures and leaflets are produced. In particular, you should now know the significance of the number of pages you choose. You will also appreciate that the more colour you use, the higher the cost. This will perhaps get you thinking creatively about design as well as copywriting.

You have also practised writing brochure copy and have discovered the power of rhetorical questioning to stop your reader reading and start them thinking. Design and the use of tables can then focus their attention where it will influence them most.

Distributing printed material is best done with a covering letter and, as you have seen, while that letter needs to be written by you, it could be printed on someone more influential's letterhead and also bear their signature.

SUNDAY

MONDAY

TUESDAY

WEDNESDAY

THURSDAY

FRIDAY

SATURDAY

Fact-check (answers at the back)

1. Asking questions, that you then answer, makes brochure copy:
   a) Easier to write ❑
   b) Easier to break up into manageable chunks ❑
   c) Easier for your reader to understand and follow ❑
   d) Easier to proof-read ❑

2. The best promotional copy illustrates how what you're offering:
   a) Is the only option on the market so like it or go without ❑
   b) Is relevant to each reader's ability, aspiration and interest ❑
   c) Is amazingly cheap ❑
   d) Is technically complex, but people soon get the hang of it ❑

3. Features are what something is and benefits what it:
   a) Might once have been ❑
   b) Can do for the buyer ❑
   c) Is made of ❑
   d) Does for you as the provider ❑

4. A conversational style of copywriting will:
   a) Appear overly familiar to many and so is best avoided ❑
   b) Contain lots of slang or jargon to show your knowledge ❑
   c) Build good rapport with the reader and hold their interest ❑
   d) Encourage you to use lots of words you don't usually speak ❑

5. Captions under the pictures in your brochures will:
   a) Make it clear what you want people to focus on ❑
   b) Present opportunities for humour ❑
   c) Waste space best used for more detailed information ❑
   d) Confuse people ❑

6. A covering letter sent with a brochure:
   a) Is neater than simply putting a label on the envelope ❑
   b) Allows you to personalize the mailing to each recipient ❑
   c) Is not really that important ❑
   d) Overcomplicates the task ❑

7. The best way to prompt a positive response is to insert:
   a) A personal plea for support ❑
   b) A promotional mouse-mat so they can order online ❑
   c) Your business card ❑
   d) A pre-completed order form with a time limited offer ❑

8. A clever way to add weight to your sales information is to: ❑
   a) Wrap the brochure round a brick ❑
   b) Enclose an endorsement by someone well-known ❑
   c) Send two brochures, so people can share them ❑
   d) Print it on heavier paper ❑

9. Enclosing a survey form, perhaps with an incentive to return it:
   a) Is a great way to find out how your organization is regarded ❑
   b) Gives you the chance to get better at preparing spreadsheets ❑

103

c) Is a waste of time when you can email a link to an online survey instead ❏

d) Won't work unless you include a pen and reply paid envelope ❏

10. It's not what you say that matters most, it's:

a) The fact you can back up the message with hard facts ❏

b) The way that you say it ❏

c) Who you send it to ❏

d) How many words you use ❏

SUNDAY

MONDAY

TUESDAY

WEDNESDAY

THURSDAY

FRIDAY

SATURDAY

SATURDAY

Composing proposals and presentation visuals

The last section of this copywriting book is a good place to cover as many as possible of the copywriting opportunities not mentioned so far. Of course, there is not the space to explore every opportunity, but here are a few specific types of copywriting you might find particularly useful.

Today, therefore, you will:

Practise writing proposals

Appreciate how to write for PowerPoint™

Consider the importance of effective signage

Recognize the opportunities that vehicle livery presents

Proposals

After the sales letter, the follow-up brochure and a successful sales presentation, the proposal is often the next piece of copywriting you need. It could be argued that all proposals are sales documents; they certainly are written to prompt a positive response.

Remember the importance of sticking to the three key objectives when planning your proposal. You may recall that these are what you want your reader to **know**, **think** and **do** as a result of reading your words. Within the context of a proposal, it is important to be quite explicit, so for example if you are recommending an investment in your IT support service, you might choose to include:

Know	The size of your team and how they provide remote 24/7 cover Your estimation (using the customer's figures) of the cost of downtime Your charges, what is included and what is extra
Think	That your proposal represents good value for money That you are big enough to provide the cover and response times you are promising That your existing customers are happy with your service
Do	Agree to the contract you are proposing

When writing a proposal, you need to remember that your reader is expecting (and has in fact agreed to receive) the information you are sharing. They have expressed interest in what you can do and need reassuring that what you propose will meet their needs. Whether your proposal is one of several on the table or the only one, you must be sure to answer each of the points raised.

The best proposals are concise, specific and easy to read. Information that supports your arguments can always be placed at the back of the document, in an appendix, but always aim to keep the main document to four pages or fewer. To achieve this you can:

● Use bullet points
   - To provide the facts without embellishment
   - To make reading (and rereading) easy

- Use footnotes
  - Footnotes can either expand on the point you are making or, better, refer the reader to an appendix
- Use tables
  - To summarize and provide comparative data
  - Graphs can be even better, but do also give the figures
- Number pages
  - You can also number paragraphs, but this suggests the document is already becoming too long

Structure

If you write a lot of proposals you can save yourself time by sticking to a common structure. However, do resist the temptation to create a new proposal by simply opening and editing one you prepared earlier. This causes the meaning and focus of the document to decay a little each time you do it, and you also run the risk of committing the cardinal sin of the proposal writer: forgetting to delete copy that is specific to the proposal on which you are basing this one. It is a common problem and one that loses customers. No one wants to buy a second-hand idea.

The best way is to create a proposal template that not only gives you a common structure but a common style too. Here are some possible headings.

- Background – why the proposal is being written. A chance to reflect your version of the brief to demonstrate you understand
- Challenge – two or three bullet points that summarize the need
- Opportunity – two or three bullet points that summarize your solution
- Activity – how your solution will work, step by step
- Benefits – what the activity delivers and what it's worth
- Budget – what it's all going to cost
- Next? – call to action. Introduce urgency if possible

Language

Clearly it is important to use language that your reader is comfortable with but try to make frequent use of the words *you* and *your* and, in almost every case, write it as if you (the writer) are making a proposal directly, one-to-one. This implies that you are taking responsibility and ownership. Writing in a corporate style ('we recommend'), while it suggests a degree of collaboration has taken place, is not as powerful as a personal plea.

Now it's time for you to try this approach yourself. Write a proposal that recommends that your boss buys each of your team a copy of this book. Make the proposal no more than 600 words long. Think what the business benefits could be if everyone became a more effective writer.

PowerPoint™ presentations

PowerPoint™ has made it easy for everyone to use colourful slides to illustrate their presentations. However, too many people simply use it to reproduce their notes on the screen. Here are six top tips for using PowerPoint™:

- Colour – keep things simple and always put dark text on light backgrounds. Avoid strident colours, be conservative
- Text – large, clear, not all capital letters. Words, not sentences
- Questions – questions on the screen can focus the audience
- Pictures – pictures and a few words are better than either alone
- Animation – special effects detract from the message. Avoid them
- Sound/video – sound and video clips can be powerful, but only if good recordings. Let the speaker do the talking!

Remember too that you use PowerPoint™ to support, not replace or upstage your presentation. Keep your slides simple. This will make your message clearer with less risk of technical errors distracting you and your audience.

Signage

If you operate a retail outlet, or simply have a site with lots of people, you will appreciate the value of effective signage. At locations such as hospitals, where people may be unfamiliar with the place and also be distressed, signage has become a science. Here are some pointers to help you:

● Clarity – signs should be easy to read, perhaps also illustrated
● Brevity – use as few words as possible
● Sell benefits – for example: *free range* eggs, *great value* cars, *bargain* books (selling signs are like advertising headlines)
● Avoid negatives – even prohibiting signs can be positive. 'Access required 24/7' is nicer than 'No parking'

Perhaps the most creative copywriting opportunity can be found on vehicles. This is because you can:

● Use humour – play on your company name or product benefit, and link to the fact that the words appear on a vehicle
● Use shape – you can cheaply cover a whole vehicle with lettering
● Use mirror image – reverse words on the front of a vehicle, so that they read 'properly' in a rear view mirror
● Use your vehicles as travelling advertisements – the technology exists to reproduce your advertising on, say, the back of a lorry. If you're selling to consumers – don't miss the opportunity

What you will see from these last few copywriting applications is that whatever you write, wherever it will be read, there are common-sense rules that are common to all. Once you start to think about it, there will be countless opportunities to deliver your product, service or corporate values message to those you wish to influence. In many instances, those messages will be the same. If you are writing material for internal consumption within a large organization, it should ideally reflect the commitments offered to customers.

As you develop your copywriting skills, you may find that you discover a passion for the power of influence our words can wield on our behalf. Reading widely, experimenting with form, content and shape will all help you develop your skills. The real key to success is experience. The more you write, the easier it will become. Practice makes perfect. Now it's down to you to seek perfection. Enjoy!

Summary

Today we've looked at a number of applications for your creative copywriting. We've looked at how even internal documents such as reports and proposals need to sell. In fact, everything you write has to have a clear purpose, even if it's only to entertain.

With PowerPoint™ we illustrated the fact that fewer words can often mean more meaning. Your reader is always going to be pressed for time, not least when trying to listen to you as well as read your slides.

Lastly we looked at signs. These, you will recall, are situations where you have no influence over the reader, other than by catching their eye.

This final chapter, by covering more of the practical applications of copywriting, provides an opportunity. You see while the book has encouraged you to write with more focus, clarity and purpose, there are three quite different relationships you will have with your reader:

When you write a report or proposal, you have the reader in mind.

SUNDAY

MONDAY

TUESDAY

WEDNESDAY

THURSDAY

FRIDAY

SATURDAY

When you prepare a presentation, you may know who's going to be there, but often you don't. You do, however, have the opportunity to speak to them and influence the way they interpret what you've written.

And signage, like advertising, has to work all on its own. You don't know who is going to see it or how they are going to respond. This is the situation where your words will have to work the hardest.

Now you're at the end of the book. We have run out of words for you to read. It's time for you to start writing some yourself. Good luck!

Fact-check (answers at the back)

1. Proposals are important selling documents; they need to be:
   a) Concise and explicit with evidence to support your argument ❑
   b) Emotional, demonstrating your passion for the project ❑
   c) Comprehensive, covering all the options in detail ❑
   d) Short and simple ❑

2. A good way to make a proposal easy to navigate is to use:
   a) Lots of different colours ❑
   b) Graphics, so the whole thing becomes a large diagram ❑
   c) The covering letter to suggest the reader allows plenty of time to read and digest the document ❑
   d) Bullet points and simple graphs to illustrate key statistics ❑

3. You'll save a lot of time when writing proposals if you create:
   a) Each in a different way ❑
   b) A common template you can adapt to any situation ❑
   c) A standard company presentation into which you insert a few points mentioned in the invitation to tender ❑
   d) A team and share out the preparation ❑

4. The best PowerPoint presentations:
   a) Are full of strident colours and animation ❑
   b) Have lots of writing you can read with your audience ❑
   c) Are simple with few words and striking images ❑

   d) Use the full array of PowerPoint features ❑

5. Signs works best when they:
   a) Show the benefit as well as the feature – 'free range eggs' ❑
   b) Are filled with text ❑
   c) Are printed in a lurid DayGlo® background ❑
   d) Move ❑

And here are five questions to set you off in the right direction as you further develop your copywriting skills.

6. The best way to continue to develop your copywriting skills is to:
   a) Buy more books on copywriting ❑
   b) Keep on writing and stretch yourself creatively ❑
   c) Study English grammar ❑
   d) Get a mentor better at writing than you ❑

7. The best way to broaden your vocabulary is to:
   a) Buy a dictionary and read a few pages every evening ❑
   b) Carry a notebook and write down words you hear but don't understand ❑
   c) Do crosswords (not the cryptic ones) ❑
   d) Watch TV quiz shows ❑

8. Some of the greatest authors in the world started out as:
   a) Van drivers ❑
   b) Copywriters ❑
   c) Plumbers ❑
   d) CEOs ❑

115

9. When people criticize your writing they are actually:
a) Helping you understand how readers interpret your words ☐
b) Idiots, jealous of your achievement ☐
c) Probably better at it than you
d) After your job ☐

10. Robert Ashton, the author of this book:
a) Hates hearing from readers ☐
b) Never answers emails ☐
c) Is unapproachable ☐
d) Welcomes feedback and comments at robert@ robertashton.co.uk ☐

Surviving in tough times

Right now you have to get it 'write' first time. Times are tough and nobody's got the time to re-read what at first glance is confusing or wide of the mark.

Words have to work really hard. And so do you if you are going to influence others with what you write. Remember it's not about grammar; it's about meaning.

This book will help you write more clearly and concisely, enabling you to compress complex information into language anyone can understand.

Become more confident; become better understood; become part of your organization's future, not its past!

1 Put on your readers' spectacles

You know what you want to say. But these days you need to know what your reader wants to see. Glance at the world through your readers' spectacles, then use words they'll understand to introduce them to the fresh perspective you're providing. And if their spectacles are smeary, cut through the haze with your powerful, punchy prose.

2 Paint word pictures

Use verbal metaphor to paint word pictures in people's minds. If their world looks like a battlefield, with shellfire and smoke, your words must provide shelter, perhaps even escape!

The skilful use of metaphor can also make people smile. In times when there's little to laugh about, if your words cheer, you'll achieve your goals more easily. Now that'll be something to cheer about!

3 Stand out from the crowd

It could be a CV or a proposal for investment in your department. Today more than ever the documents you present have to stand out from the crowd.

Don't be afraid to use colour, shape and, most importantly, pictures to make your work leap out of the pile. Get noticed, be shortlisted and then win the day.

These are times when it pays to be different and anything but the same.

4 Say it like it is

There really is no substitute for cutting to the chase and saying it like it is. Your writing needs to be direct, specific and explicit. Only then will you hold attention and lead your reader down to the punchline. Time is short, so avoid euphemisms and get straight to the point.

5 What's in it for me?

Most business communication is by email or online messaging. Your subject line will be all that's read before the decision is made: 'Do I open or delete?'. People are pressed for time and will open your message only if you give them a good reason to do so.

Remember to keep it businesslike; juicy ham, not spam!

6 It pays to advertise – do it!

Advertising works, but only if you remember to say what it is, who it's for, why it's a good deal. Add urgency with a 'when', and tell people how to buy.

No budget for this? Don't worry, this title shows you how to make classified advertising work and even how to advertise for free. Go on, flaunt it and win.

7 Adopt a journalist today!

The media are in a tough place too. Rising print costs and falling ad revenue means that journalists need friends like you.

The easier you make life for the journalists in your business sector, the more of your stories they'll run. Read how to structure a news release, make it current, urgent and even newsworthy.

8 Talk benefits not features

Only geeks care about how things are made and what makes them tick. Most folk just want to know what your product or service will do for them. Write about the benefits and make them personal.

It's not just in marketing you need to sell benefits. You'll get problems fixed quicker if you sell the benefits of pushing your issue to the top of the pile.

9 Put your writing on the wall

Nobody wants to read a wordy Powerpoint presentation; they've all got better things to do, especially these days. Simple, big and bold is what will burn your message into people's brains. You can then set the scene and answer questions.

Today, people want interaction. Then they'll feel part of what it is you're suggesting is good for them to do. Remember: less is more!

10 Make sure people see the sign

Signage can do much more than warn of hazards or point out the loo. Shortcut those lengthy briefings and put the message on the wall instead. Even in the loo if you like!

Read on and learn how to write signs that motivate as well as inform. Signs can be fun too – and that makes them all the more memorable.

Answers

Sunday: 1b; 2c; 3c; 4a; 5d; 6c; 7a; 8d; 9c; 10a
Monday: 1b; 2b; 3a; 4b; 5c; 6b; 7a; 8c; 9c; 10a
Tuesday: 1c; 2b; 3a; 4d; 5a; 6c; 7a; 8c; 9c; 10a
Wednesday: 1c; 2c; 3a; 4d; 5d; 6d; 7a; 8a; 9b; 10d
Thursday: 1d; 2b; 3a; 4c; 5b; 6b; 7c; 8a; 9b; 10d
Friday: 1c; 2b; 3b; 4c; 5a; 6b; 7d; 8b; 9a; 10b
Saturday: 1a; 2d; 3b; 4c; 5a; 6b; 7c; 8b; 9a; 10d

Notes

LEARN IN A WEEK,
WHAT THE EXPERTS
LEARN IN A LIFETIME

For information about other titles
in the series, please visit
www.inaweek.co.uk